TWENTIETH CENTURY INTERPRETATIONS

OF

NATIVE SON

A Collection of Critical Essays

Edited by

Houston A. Baker, Jr.

Prentice-Hall, Inc.   *Englewood Cliffs, N.J.*

A SPECTRUM BOOK

Library of Congress Cataloging in Publication Data

BAKER, HOUSTON A   comp.
   Twentieth century interpretations of Native son.

   (Twentieth century interpretations) (A Spectrum book)
   CONTENTS: Wright, R. How "Bigger" was born.—Baldwin, J. Many thousands gone.—Howe, I. Black boys and native sons. [etc.]
   1. Wright, Richard, 1908-1960. Native son.
I. Title.
PS3545.R815N33   813'.5'2   72-8136
ISBN 0-13-609982-3
ISBN 0-13-609974-2 (pbk.)

Quotations from *Native Son* used by permission of Harper & Row, Publishers, Inc. and Jonathan Cape Limited. Copyright 1940 by Richard Wright; renewed, 1968 by Ellen Wright.

Printed in the United States of America.
10   9   8   7   6   5   4   3   2   1

PRENTICE-HALL INTERNATIONAL, INC. (*London*)
PRENTICE-HALL OF AUSTRALIA, PTY. LTD. (*Sydney*)
PRENTICE-HALL OF CANADA, LTD. (*Toronto*)
PRENTICE-HALL OF INDIA PRIVATE LIMITED (*New Delhi*)
PRENTICE-HALL OF JAPAN, INC. (*Tokyo*)

88202

Contents

To Mark

Introduction

by Houston A. Baker, Jr.

There could hardly have been a more divergent pair than Ellen Wilson, a fair-skinned, literate, and retiring woman, and Nathan Wright, a powerful, dark, and uneducated sharecropper from Mississippi's Upper Delta. Yet Ellen and Nathan were married in 1907, and a year later, on September 4, when Nathan found himself deeper in debt to the plantation owner who furnished the essentials of his tenancy, Richard Wright was born. His birthplace was Natchez, but his life was more influenced by his early migrations than by any one specific place of birth or residence. According to Blyden Jackson, the character of Wright's life proceeded from the masses of America's "Black Belt," a dense Southern body that has thinned since the turn of the century and become the mass of America's "urban ghettos." [1] During his first nineteen years, Wright was nurtured on the values, modes of adaptation, patterns of social and religious organization, bitterness, aspirations, violence, and cuisine of the Southern black American folk. And during these years he moved from Natchez to Memphis, from Memphis to Jackson, Mississippi, from Jackson to Elaine, Arkansas, and from Elaine back to Jackson, where he completed the ninth grade of Smith-Robertson Public School in 1925. The next move was to Memphis, and here the young boy worked until he had earned enough money to depart from the Southern black folk and join the northern in the "promised land" of the American city. It is a dynamic, flowing pattern, which Wright reduced to its essentials in *Black Boy*, an autobiography published in 1945.

Hunger, fear, a father who deserted the family, the violence of

---

"*Racial Wisdom and Richard Wright's* Native Son" *by Houston A. Baker, Jr., from* Long Black Song: Essays in Black American Literature and Culture (*Charlottesville: University Press of Virginia, 1972*), *pp. 122–41. Reprinted by permission of University Press of Virginia.*

[1] Blyden Jackson, "Richard Wright: Black Boy From America's Black Belt and Urban Ghettos," *CLA Journal*, XII (June, 1969), 287–309.

whites who killed one of his uncles in order to take over his property, the malignity of a sporting "professor" who was courting his
aunt and who murdered a white woman with whom he was having
an affair and burned the house that contained her lifeless body,
these were but a few of the grim elements of Wright's early life.
There was also the domineering Uncle Tom who once advanced on
his young relative with a switch:

> "I've got a razor in each hand!" I warned in a low, charged
> voice. "If you touch me, I'll cut you, so help me God!"
> He paused, staring at my lifted hands in the dawning light of
> morning. I held a sharp blue-edge of steel tightly between thumb
> and forefinger of each fist.
> "My God," he gasped.[2]

Violence was omnipresent: there were beatings by whites, black
women raped, black men fighting back as "bad niggers," black men
castrated and lynched. Squalor, fanaticism, and fear characterized
the decaying black tenements of Southern cities. And a grandmother's overzealous devotion to the Seventh-Day Adventist Church
left as much of an imprint on Wright's early years as the custom-
ridden relations between black men and white women. The primary element of his life, however, and of all black lives in America,
in the words of Stephen Henderson, was "survival motion." [3]
    The principal of Smith-Robertson considered Wright an out-
standing student, and the editor of Jackson's *Southern Register*
accepted a melodramatic short story, "The Voodoo of Hell's Half-
Acre," in 1924 and encouraged the author to continue writing;
these were two bright spots in a world of leanness and neglect. The
young man left the South, however, with more than he conceived.
From his first screams in a sharecropper's cabin to his stealthy
escape by night from Jackson, he had been bathed in the culture
of the black American folk; he rode a night train to Chicago as a
man imbued with the concepts, skills, arts, and institutions of
America's black folk population.
    The northern phase of Wright's life did nothing toward the de-

    [2] Richard Wright, *Black Boy* (New York: Signet, 1963), p. 175. All citations
from *Black Boy* in my text refer to this edition.
    [3] Stephen E. Henderson, " 'Survival Motion' A Study of the Black Writer and
the Black Revolution in America," in *The Militant Black Writer in Africa and
the United States,* eds. Mercer Cook and Stephen E. Henderson (Madison, Wisconsin: University of Wisconsin Press, 1969), pp. 63–129.

culturation of the young man of twenty who arrived in Chicago on a chill December day and made his way to an enclave of black urban culture. His experiences in Chicago and New York for the next twenty years simply reinforced the fundamental attitudes and assumptions he had acquired in the South. Here in the North also were hunger, "Negro jobs," black population density, intra- and inter-racial violence, decaying tenements, resentful blacks, and prejudiced whites. The environment altered the modes of adaptation of the folk, but the primary goal and driving impetus of black life was the same as in the South—survival, by any means necessary.

Of course, there is no need to minimize the genuine broadening that Wright underwent in social, intellectual, artistic, and economic spheres during the thirties and forties. The process of self-education that he had begun while working for an optical firm in Memphis continued when he moved to Chicago. Here he did not have to borrow a white man's library card or forge a note saying, "Dear Madam: Will you please let this nigger boy have some books by H. L. Mencken," [4] but he did have to move beyond the boundaries of his own ghetto environment in order to obtain the type of intellectual stimulation he desired. The John Reed Club of Chicago (an organization of radical artists and writers) and the Communist Party of America seemed to promise this stimulation. The John Reed Clubs were nationally organized by the Communist Party in 1932, and by March of the following year Wright was not only Executive Secretary of the Chicago branch but also an official member of the Party. The writers associated with these clubs throughout the country were some of the most noted in white and black American literature: John Dos Passos, Langston Hughes, Theodore Dreiser, Malcolm Cowley, and others. Under the auspices and tutelage of the John Reed Club and the Party, Wright produced poetry, essays, and fiction dedicated to the melioration of world social conditions. His intellectual and social vision expanded to include the lowly and oppressed from all points of the compass, and he genuinely believed (and there are "many thousands gone" who did likewise) that the Communist Party was committed to the cause of civil rights for the black man in America.

The Communist experience for Wright, however, was more than dedication and social vision. Early in his encounters with the Party, he felt that he could enjoy warm and sincere human relationships

---

[4] Wright, *Black Boy*, p. 270.

for the first time in his life. Jan Wittenberger (surely the model for
Jan Erlone in *Native Son*), who recruited Wright for the John Reed
Club was undoubtedly the person who reinforced this view of human relations in the Party. Considering his life as a whole, in fact,
one can see that communism was an ideology that fitted Wright's
fundamental cultural assumptions rather than a political camp for
which he had to remold his life and values. A communal or col-
lectivistic ethos has always characterized black culture in America,
distinguishing it unequivocally from white American culture. The
latter endorses individualism and self-help as roads to advancement,
but black Americans have long known (as David Walker's *Appeal*,
1829, and Henry Highland Garnet's "Address to the Slaves of the
United States," 1843, demonstrate) that there can be no advancement of the black individual until the social, economic, and political codes of society have been altered in a manner that makes possible the upward mobility of the entire body of black Americans.
Seldom, for all too patent reasons, have black Americans viewed
society as a protective arena in which the individual can work out
his own destiny.

To understand the basis in black culture for Wright's "natural
allegiance" to the Communist Party helps to elucidate the theme
and structure of both *Uncle Tom's Children* (a collection of four
novellas published in 1938 and reissued with the addition of
"Bright and Morning Star" and "The Ethics of Living Jim Crow"
in 1940) and *Native Son* (Wright's first novel, published by Harper
and Brothers in 1940) to a greater degree than does a critical perspective grounded in Marxist ideology. The group which provided
(in Sainte-Beuve's phrase) "all the maturing and value" for Richard
Wright, also suggested the strategies of survival and conditioned
the world view that he set forth in literature. In one of the most
ideological stories in *Uncle Tom's Children*, "Fire and Cloud," it
is not communism that wins the day for Reverend Taylor and his
congregation; it is rather a fused strength based on black religion
and reinforced by the belief that not God but "the black people"
should receive one's sincerest tributes.[5] In the other stories of
Uncle Tom's Children, this same sense of fused strength is evident:
an affirmation of the positive good to be derived from the unifica-
tion of black people to overcome their oppressors. The theme of
the volume, "freedom belongs to the strong," certainly implies

[5] Richard Wright, *Uncle Tom's Children* (New York: Signet, 1963), p. 156.

that Wright believed a united black community stabilized by shared cultural assumptions had the greatest chance of achieving freedom.

In *Native Son,* Bigger Thomas dreams of a strong black man who will emerge to unite the black people. The fulfillment of his dream, of course, is Bigger himself. Accepting the whole way of life that is his culture, at the end of the novel he emerges as the same type of existential character we see in autobiographical accounts of black American slaves. A case in point is offered by the *Narrative of William Wells Brown, a Fugitive Slave.* One of the most memorable sequences in this narrative records the stages of Brown's physical and psychological movement away from his owners and across the state of Ohio to freedom. Having reclaimed the name of "William," which his master took from him, and repudiated "trust" and "honor" as defined by his master ("Servants, obey your masters"), he sits cold and alone by a makeshift fire, eating stolen ears of corn, but feeling "all right." Bigger's movement from bondage to freedom follows the same course: he repudiates white American culture, affirms black survival values, and serves as a model hero—a strong man getting stronger, to use Sterling Brown's words—for all readers of *Native Son* who possess the culture which provided maturation and value for its author.

There is a *necessary* distinction to be made between Wright's works and the works of the Proletarian School of the thirties and forties. While it is true that Wright was influenced by the naturalism and polemical concerns of his contemporaries, it is also true that his use of naturalism was not the ideologically and literarily self-conscious choice made by such men as John Dos Passos, Mike Gold, and John Steinbeck. Comparing Wright's life with that of almost any of Emile Zola's protagonists, one immediately recognizes the similarity. Wright's existence in the Black Belt and the urban ghettos of America was one in which events seemed predetermined by heredity (the simple fact of melanin), and the environment seemed under some sort of divine injunction to destroy. Wright's choice of communism on an ideological plane and of naturalism on a literary plane were, in part, culturally determined, and they led to works that mark a highpoint in the black American literary tradition. One cannot apply critical censures designed for American proletarian literature to Wright's work without modification. The following statement by Nathan Scott serves to illustrate:

And, however robust our respect may still be for the Dos Passos of the *U.S.A.* trilogy or the Steinbeck of *The Grapes of Wrath* or the Wright of *Native Son,* we find them today to be writers with whom it is virtually impossible any longer to have a genuinely reciprocal relation, for the simple fact is that the rhetoric of what once used to be called "reportage" proves itself, with the passage of time, to be a language lacking in the kind of amplitude and resonance that *lasts.* This may not be the precise judgment which the cunning of history, in its ultimate justice, will sustain, but it is, at any rate, *ours.*[6]

Without entertaining the "ultimate," it seems apparent that such a generalized formula is not applicable to Wright. The most significant niche is scarcely to be found in the Proletarian School.

When his comrades in the Communist Party increased his anxieties by ominous hints of purges in Moscow and talk of the fate of "bastard intellectuals" and "incipient Trotskyites" in their midst, Wright realized that he did not belong in the Marxist gallery. In 1937 his "Fire and Cloud" had won *Story* magazine's prize for the best short story of the year; 1939 brought him a Guggenheim fellowship; and in 1940 *Native Son* was chosen as a Book-of-the-Month Club selection, and he was awarded the Spingarn Medal by the National Association for the Advancement of Colored People. As an established author, he now asserted his artistic prerogatives and was more than miffed when the Party criticized *Native Son* for—of all things—its individualism and failure to portray the black and white masses of America. In the early forties the Party had also shifted its policies toward the American Negro; no longer was the granting of full citizenship rights to black Americans to be a goal. By the end of 1943, therefore, Wright had withdrawn from it. In 1944 he published "I Tried to Be a Communist" and five years later contributed an essay to Richard Crossman's *The God That Failed,* a collection of essays reflecting the disenchantment of former Communist supporters.

During the early forties Wright had made even more fundamental shifts in his status. In 1940 he married a ballet dancer, whom he divorced after they had spent an extended (but, for

---

[6] Nathan A. Scott, Jr., "The Dark and Haunted Tower of Richard Wright," in *Black Expression,* ed. Addison Gayle, Jr. (New York: Horizon Press, 1969), p. 308.

Wright, all too "bourgeois") season in Mexico, and in 1941 he married Ellen Poplar, a white member of the Communist Party in New York. In effect, the dream with which he leaves his readers at the end of *Black Boy* had come true: he had achieved fame and stability as a writer (the earnings from his writings totalled thirty thousand dollars), he had married the woman he loved, and his daughter Julia, born in 1942, was moving into a beautiful and precocious childhood. But living in New York has never been easy for a black man, and when an invitation to visit France was extended by the French government, Wright promptly accepted. Soon after his return, while walking the streets of Greenwich Village one day and marvelling at the abundance of America, he paused before a small store's display, then decided to buy some fruit to take home. While he was making his selection, the Italian owner rushed out of the store and brusquely asked, "Whudda yuh want, boy?" With the question, Wright's feeling of a moment before—"It's like Christmas! Just like Christmas!"—vanished, and once again he was suffering the "old and ancient agonies" at the hands of his white American neighbors. One individual from what Ellison calls "the waves of immigrants who have come later and passed us by" had made Wright acutely aware of his true culture. His white neighbors on Charles Street were not the least bit kinder; on occasion, the word "Nigger," spoken distinctly and loudly enough for him to hear, drifted from a group of white gossipers as he climbed the steps to his home. After a short and frustrating stay in the United States, therefore, he departed once more for France and never again saw his native land.

The last thirteen years of his life were full ones; they were charged with new experiences, interesting friendships, approval as well as indifference for his works, hope for an emerging Africa and a dying colonialism, a feeling of awe before an advanced technology, French existentialism (which accorded with Wright's modes of interpreting experience), new world leaders, and his own possessive involvement with his family—the brilliant Julia, energetic Rachel (a second daughter born in 1949), and devoted Ellen. In "Alas, Poor Richard," [7] James Baldwin (a sensitive observer by any standard) characterizes Wright's Paris years as a time of disillusionment and surliness, but one does not receive the same impression

[7] James Baldwin, "Alas, Poor Richard," in *Nobody Knows My Name* (New York: Dell, 1968), pp. 146–70.

from Constance Webb's *Richard Wright*.[8] Possibly an understanding of Baldwin's Oedipal rage and unhappiness because his artistic *pater familias* could not be easily purged from his psyche should lead us to place more faith in Miss Webb's assessment.

The works of the last years, from *The Outsider* (a novel, 1953) to *Eight Men* (a collection of short stories prepared for publication in 1960 but published posthumously in 1961), reflect Wright's attempts to continue his self-education and to order in some way the swiftly changing world around him. Africa and Asia seemed to him (as they had to W. E. B. Du Bois more than a half century earlier) to hold both a threat and a promise for the modern world, and he explored the complexities of the color line and the new "tragic elite" (leaders of former colonial territories) in *Black Power* (a report on his visit to the Gold Coast, 1954) and *The Color Curtain* (a report on the Asian Bandung Conference, 1956). Spain also was an attractive yet baffling country, and following his instincts and curiosity he visited it twice in an attempt to order his initial reactions; *Pagan Spain* (1956) was the result. Ever since the Civil War of the thirties, Spain had proved a fertile subject for contemporary writers, but Wright's view was conditioned by his own background. He understood the mentality of the Spanish peasant, and this, coupled with his knowledge of the social, theological, and economic patterns of an industrial world, make *Pagan Spain* an insightful and provocative book.

The creative works of the last years include *Savage Holiday* (1954) and *The Long Dream* (1958). Both novels deal with the condition of contemporary man in an exploitative world, but neither met with even a mild critical success. In part, this cool reception (indifferent in the case of *Savage Holiday*) was justified. The books are not candidates for rave reviews, and in both there is a tension between a metaphysical rebellion (which was much more forceful in Wright's cathartic years of the thirties and forties than in the early fifties) and a broad, humanistic view of the Western world. The attempted unity is ambitious and commendable, but finally

---

[8] Constance Webb, *Richard Wright, A Biography* (New York: G. P. Putnam's Sons, 1968). This work is at present the most definitive biography of Wright; the book is sensitive, intelligent, and well-written. It is one of the few biographical accounts from which the reader receives a genuine feeling for the subject, and I have relied heavily on it for anecdotal and pedagogical information concerning Wright. John A. Williams' *The Most Native of Sons* (Garden City, N.Y.: Doubleday and Company, 1970) offers a straightforward, high-school level approach to Wright's life.

the tension is neither sustained nor resolved in the fine artistic manner displayed in the author's best fiction. Another novel, *Lawd Today* (begun in 1934 but published posthumously), has done little to enhance his reputation. The later works are at times exciting, however, and they deserve more critical attention than they have received from American critics, who curiously seem to feel that the end of Wright's artistic life coincides with his departure from the United States in 1947.

On November 28, 1960, after three days of tests at the Clinique Chirugicale Eugéne Gibez in Paris, Richard Wright, like his most famous protagonist, was feeling "all right." According to the tests, his health was apparently fine. During the early evening he had read all of the newspapers, but after placing the book that he was reading on the bedside table, he felt a sharp pain and reached out his hand for the signal light.

> Three minutes later the floor nurse came out of another patient's room, looked up the hallway and saw Richard's light. She walked quietly in her rubber-soled shoes to his room and entered. Richard lay on his back, his head turned toward the door, an apologetic smile on his lips as though to excuse himself for disturbing her. Before he could speak he simply seemed to fall away, his face smoothed of lines. Richard Wright was dead at fifty-two years of age.[9]

Possibly Wright's apologetic smile had as much to do with the absurdity of his dying when he had so many plans as with his feelings toward the nurse. An ambitious, searching, and strong man, his works seldom manifest anything like a Freudian death urge; his protagonists are always committed to a life lived fully and wholly. There are always obstacles in their path, and they are often destroyed as a result of their commitment, but the title of a long work planned shortly before his death captures the mood of his fiction. The proposed title was "Celebration." Wright's works are generally celebrations of life, particularly the complex life lived by black Americans. Black Americans, Wright repeatedly asserts, are the affirmers; they have had every imaginable pressure exerted against them while they have continued to assert the principles of humanity vested in the American Constitution and the Bill of Rights more fully and effectively than any group on the continent. The "native son," in his eyes, could only be the

[9] Webb, *Richard Wright*, p. 399.

black American. Bigger Thomas's culture is the history of the black American, and it coincides precisely with the founding and duration of the United States. From 1619 to the present, black American culture has grown and flourished, and *Native Son* irrefutably demonstrates that Richard Wright was one of its finest artists and most sensitive chroniclers.

II

For thirty years criticism and commentary on *Native Son* have mounted: positive and negative, insightful and absurd, respectful and racist—the criticism seems to reflect the fundamental reactions of America to its own history. Thus, the aim of the protagonist has been fulfilled:

> . . . he wished that he could be an idea in their minds; that his black face and the image of his smothering Mary and cutting off her head and burning her could hover before their eyes as a terrible picture of reality which they could see and feel and yet not destroy.[10]

Bigger Thomas struck America's most vulnerable nerve; he attacked its "symbol of beauty" (p. 155), the white female. There is little mystery about *Native Son's* ability to attract successive generations of American readers; the great taboo of American culture is shattered in the book, and human beings, like Ralph Ellison's Mr. Norton in *Invisible Man,* possess a fateful desire to look upon chaos without being destroyed. It is Trueblood in *Invisible Man,*[11] however, who actually has vision, and in Wright's novel it is Bigger Thomas. Mr. Norton remains sightless, and those surrounding Bigger (Mrs. Dalton and even the sympathetic lawyer, Boris Max) remain blind.

There is some irony in the fact that critics—black and white—search the novel's image clusters, dialogue, point of view, ideology, and allusions for the source of its power. Those who have undertaken such structural safaris have often shared Mr. Norton's and

---

[10] Richard Wright, *Native Son* (New York: Harper and Row, 1940), p. 110. All citations from *Native Son* refer to this edition.

[11] Ralph Ellison, *Invisible Man* (New York: Random House, 1952). In the Signet edition, the Norton-Trueblood encounter covers pp. 46–66.

Mrs. Dalton's fate; they have remained blind to one of the most essential sources of power. Codes restricting the alliance of blacks and whites in colonial America, a Civil War, anti-miscegenation laws, thousands of lynchings, the murder of Emmett Till—all point to one reason for *Native Son*'s force; all of these manifestations of American culture reinforce Bigger's belief that Mary Dalton and her kin are "the flowers" of American civilization, the symbols of purity and innocence which the country has sought to protect. A young white female suffocated, decapitated, and cast into a roaring furnace by a twenty-year-old black man who glories in his act—this is the image that remains fixed in the reader's mind. And the image is not merely melodrama or sensationalism.

Melodramatic and sensational impulses usually proceed from the exploitative regions of an author's soul; they are composed of clichés, set formulas, and exaggerations designed to manipulate the emotions of the reader. *Native Son*'s genesis goes deeper; the book comes from a region where only truth will suffice, a region into which the unpleasant facts of history intrude for honest scrutiny, a realm where myths and stereotypes dissolve and a genuine folk heritage shines forth. When Bigger forces Mary's body into the flames, his act is no more terrifying than the slave's slapping of his white mistress to frighten away an opponent. Bigger's swing of the hatchet to take off Mary's head is no more awesome than the decisive stroke with which Nat Turner took the life of his white mistress. Stackolee's fearful acts, which stop the white sheriff from coming after him, are no less daring than Bigger's resistance to the white mob that comes seeking his life, And Brer Rabbit and the hero of the "John Cycle"—both accomplished tricksters—would have been proud of Bigger's handling of the obtuse detective Britten and the voyeuristic reporters who come to the Dalton home in search of melodrama and sensation.

Bigger's culture is that of the black American race, and he is intelligible as a conscious literary projection of the folk hero who embodies the survival values of a culture. Tales of the trickster animal who overcomes his stronger opponents; of John, the slave who outwits his master; of the "bad nigger" (Shine, Stackolee, Dupree), who rebels against an oppressive system—all of these contribute to an understanding of Wright's protagonist. Tales of pillage and plunder, accounts of black men inflicting pain and humiliation on white women with impunity, and stories of injustices suffered by black Americans are plentiful in black folklore,

and a tale such as the following helps to illuminate the perspective
of *Native Son*:

> In a little Southern town, a mob was fixing to lynch a man when
> a very dignified old judge appeared. "Don't," he pleaded, "put a
> blot on this fair community by hasty action. The thing to do,"
> he insisted, "is to give the man a fair trial and then lynch him." [12]

The story is Bigger Thomas's, and if a representative tale from the
white-woman genre is considered, the perspective becomes even
clearer:

> You take. in the South, they always have one strong colored guy
> on all the plantations. He's given a lot of consideration by the
> boss—usually he be foreman. Can put two or three of the others
> in his back pocket.

The story goes on to tell of two such men whose masters arranged
for them to fight one another. On the day of the fight, Jim, one
of the combatants, in an attempt to frighten John, his adversary,
has his boss attach him to an iron chain staked in the ground. But
John arrives at the battling grounds, slaps his own boss's wife in
the face, and watches Jim run away:

> So the loser, Jim's master, had to pay off John's boss the three or
> four thousand dollars they'd put in a bag. Still, John's boss got mad
> about his wife being slapped. He asked John, "What was the idea
> slapping my wife?" "Well, Jim knowed if I slapped a white woman
> I'd a killed *him,* so he run." [13]

John's concluding words bring to mind the fate of Bessie Mears.
When we combine tales of injustice and white-woman tales with
stories of the bad-man hero, the picture is complete. A white sheriff
responds to Billy Lyons's mother:

> Sheriff said, My name might begin with an *s* and end with an *f,*
> But if you want that bad Stackolee you got to get him yourself.[14]

Black folklore includes countless examples of strong black men
giving "a faint, wry, bitter smile," or the final, destructive thrust
to the revered symbols of white America, and Bigger Thomas's
act is simply a continuation of this heritage.

[12] Richard M. Dorson, *American Negro Folktales* (New York: Fawcett, 1970),
p. 504.
  [13] *Ibid.,* pp. 134–35.
  [14] Arna Bontemps and Langston Hughes, eds., *The Book of Negro Folklore*
(New York: Dodd, Mead and Company, 1958), p. 362.

Why, then, have Bigger's character and action, which are built of so many traditional elements, aroused such concern? The answer is not far to seek. Genuine black folklore has seldom been considered valid literary or historical evidence by our cultural custodians. The arts of the black American folk (rural and urban) have been largely ignored, caricatured, or exploited by white America. Black music, which W. E. B. Du Bois called "the most beautiful expression of human experience born this side the seas," [15] was transformed into the croons of the minstrel tradition. The forceful idioms of black folk speech were converted into the muddled syntax and thick-lipped jargon of "Negro jokes." Bessie Smith and Louis Armstrong wailing and transcending in the cabarets of Harlem became Paul Whiteman and George Gershwin harmonizing in theatres downtown. In short, the art of black folk culture (like the art of other American subcultures, such as the Irish, Italian, and Jewish) has been adjusted to suit the needs of white America—to reinforce stereotypes and sometimes even to justify the victimization of the black American. America at large has seldom taken an honest look at its black citizenry.

Since black Americans were kept illiterate by the laws of the land during much of their history, they could not challenge the general American view of the black man in poetry or prose. And when black writers did take pen in hand, polemical demands (the need to castigate slavery and caste in America) and the bare formal requirements of their craft exerted pressures that relegated the true folk heritage to a somewhat minor role. This does not mean that the folk heritage was forgotten; James Weldon Johnson's *The Autobiography of an Ex-Colored Man,* Jean Toomer's *Cane,* Langston Hughes's *Not Without Laughter,* and Arna Bontemps's *Black Thunder* all rely on the folk experience. But Richard Wright's *Native Son* was the first black novel that captured its full scope and dimension.

Wright's message to America might be stated as "we are a unique people who have produced heroes who hate and wish to destroy those contrived symbols of your culture that insure our victimization." Bigger says to his lawyer:

> "What I killed for must've been good! . . . It must have been good! When a man kills, it's for something. . . . I didn't know I

---

[15] W. E. B. Du Bois, *The Souls of Black Folk, Three Negro Classics,* ed. John Hope Franklin (New York: Avon, 1969), p. 378.

was really alive in this world until I felt things hard enough to kill for 'em. . . . It's the truth, Mr. Max. I can say it now, 'cause I'm going to die. I know what I'm saying real good and I know how it sounds. But I'm all right. I feel all right when I look at it that way. . . ." (Wright's ellipses, p. 358)

The voices of David Walker, Nat Turner, Frederick Douglass, Martin Delaney, and a dishevelled group of black forced laborers singing "Lookin' for Jimbo/ Don' say nothin'/ Go 'head Jimbo/ Don' say nothin' " [16] resound through Bigger's words. The message is simple: reverberating through black folk culture it says, "Mean mean mean to be free." [17] Both Wright's theme and hero, therefore, were drawn from the folk history to which he was heir. America's attraction to *Native Son* has been the response of the curious to the unknown, the guilty to the reason for guilt, the deceitful to exposure, the sympathetic to the oppressed, the learned to new evidence, and the perceptive to works of genius. No cultural historian (a role that Wright self-consciously assumed the year following *Native Son* in *Twelve Million Black Voices: A Folk History of the Negro in the United States*) could have hoped for more.

Irving Howe has presented a just assessment of Wright's achievement: "The day *Native Son* appeared, American culture was changed forever. No matter how much qualifying the book might later need, it made impossible a repetition of the old lies." [18] Wright brought to consummation the black artist's struggle to express a folk heritage in unequivocal terms; neither polemical demands nor the requirements of his craft distorted his portrayal of the conditions of blackness in America. In short, *Native Son* accomplished the task begun by the black intelligentsia (including Paul Laurence Dunbar, Charles Chesnutt, James Weldon Johnson, and W. E. B. Du Bois) at the turn of the century; Wright successfully translated the values of an oral tradition into written form. And the reading public's overwhelming reaction to his novel has been one of praise and discovery, shock and genuine appreciation; in the midst of white America is a culture—a whole way of life—with values in many ways antithetical to those of the

[16] Quoted from Bontemps and Hughes, eds., *Book of Negro Folklore*, "Hyah Come De Cap'm," p. 405.

[17] Robert Hayden, "Runagate Runagate," in *Selected Poems* (New York: October House, 1966), p. 77.

[18] Irving Howe, "Black Boys and Native Sons," in *A World More Attractive* (New York: Horizon Press, 1963), pp. 100–101.

larger society—symbolized by and epitomized in a five foot, nine inch black man following the example of his folk predecessors by pushing a cherished white symbol into oblivion.

III

To view Wright as a historian of black folk culture, however, raises several problems for the study of *Native Son*. In "How 'Bigger' Was Born" (1940) and again in *Black Boy,* the author seems to deny (or, at least, to disregard) the life-enhancing aspects of that culture. In "How 'Bigger' Was Born," he implies that his hero has no integral relation to it: "First, through some quirk of circumstance, he had become estranged from the religion and the folk culture of his race." [19] This statement makes one recall the conclusions about Coleridge reached by John Livingston Lowes, who after searching many possible sources of the poet's creative works was forced to admit that he could not determine precisely how these sources were transmuted into art. [20] Likewise, the manner in which Wright's experiences were transmuted into art remains unexplained even by himself. When Wright speaks of Bigger's estrangement from black folk culture and religion there is a high degree of critical myopia involved; he perceives the folk culture *in toto* as little more than folk religion. Hence, in *Native Son,* Bigger is estranged from Mrs. Thomas and Reverend Hammond (her minister), who are both symbolic projections of the author's perception of his own folk religion. Wright knew that black folk culture was more than other-worldly hymns and humble Hebraism, but in an attempt to explain the genesis of *Native Son* he did not reveal his broader wisdom.

A religious, passive, escapist life-style is presented as the essence of black American culture in "How 'Bigger' Was Born." Nevertheless, in *Native Son* Wright adopted from it several fully developed strategies that have little to do with humble passivity. From his killing of a rat in the first scene of the novel until he gives a last, bitter smile to his retreating lawyer, Bigger Thomas acts as the

[19] Richard Wright, "How 'Bigger' Was Born," *Saturday Review,* XXII (June 1, 1940), p. 4.

[20] John Livingston Lowes, *The Road to Xanadu; A Study in the Ways of the Imagination* (New York: Houghton Mifflin, 1927).

eternal man in revolt, a type of devil or bad-man hero who attempts to subvert society by refusing to heed its dictates. The burning of Mary Dalton's body and the premeditated murder of Bessie Mears are clearly the acts of a strong, Satanic figure determined, at whatever cost, to have his freedom. The moment he goes behind a mask of innocence, subservience, and stupidity to allay the suspicions of detective Britten and the newspaper reporters, Bigger plays the role of the trickster—the hero who overcomes his larger adversaries through cunning and disguise. These strategies are as important to black American folk culture as is religion. "How 'Bigger' Was Born" is an elucidating essay, but ultimately it tells us more about Wright's interpretation of *Native Son* than about the mysteries of the novel's creation. The author did not miss the mark in his attempt to create an appropriate representative of black folk culture, but his interpretation of his own paradigmatic creation is simply too narrow. There is, furthermore, a similar narrowness in *Black Boy.*

Innumerable passages in Wright's autobiography give a sense of black communality, yet the narrator denies the presence of such meaningful relations in the microcosm that he sets before the reader. There is an almost querulous insistence that his is the only sensitive, artistic, struggling soul in this world. In its projection of a creative soul out of harmony with an oppressive environment, *Black Boy* is generically akin to the slave narratives; but there is more to it. In essence, Wright's attempt at a recovery of self is more a creative than an analytical act. Regarding his Southern upbringing from the perspective of a successful author, his memory exercised a natural selectivity; out of terror, illiteracy, and oppression emerges the young, gifted, and black artist. The picture is as stirring as the autobiographer desired, for he was not reluctant to employ folk and fictional incidents in *Black Boy* for the creation of effects. Moreover, he never allows fully delineated tenderness or sentiment to distort the informing purposes of the book—to demonstrate how Richard Wright, the author, was born. In this context, Wright's much debated statements about "the essential bleakness of black life in America" come as no surprise. It would be virtually impossible to present a portrait of the *struggling* artist that delineated his culture as one which provided most of the essential elements an artist requires. The struggle for fulfillment would then become more an alternative than a necessity.

Ralph Ellison[21] and Dan McCall[22] have attempted to explain what Wright meant by his parenthetical statements on "the strange absence of real kindness" and "the cultural barrenness of black life,"[23] and if we are to consider him the chronicler of a culture, his own statements also merit our concern. The following paragraph is representative:

> Whenever I thought of the essential bleakness of black life in America, I knew that Negroes had never been allowed to catch the full spirit of Western Civilization, that they lived somehow in it but not of it. And when I brooded upon the cultural barrenness of black life, I wondered if clean, positive tenderness, love, honor, loyalty, and the capacity to remember were native with man. I asked myself if these human qualities were not fostered, won, struggled and suffered for, presented in ritual form from one generation to another. (*Black Boy*, p. 45)

Ellison regards this passage as an affirmation of black culture. Wright, according to Ellison, is pointing out that ". . . Negro sensibility is socially and historically conditioned; that Western Culture must be won, confronted like the animal in a Spanish bullfight, dominated by the red shawl of codified experience and brought heaving to its knee" (p. 103). McCall, on the other hand, feels that the passage is based on Wright's realization of the effects produced by "the terrible cultural bind of the South," which transforms the pain and desire of black life into intraracial violence. Moreover, he feels that the statement is part of the author's attempt to "find a meaning" in the bleakness, terror, lack of kindness, and violence of black life. (pp. 118–19)

Both critics provide useful explications, but neither seems to realize how fully Wright's perception of his relationship to the objective world (the world that had adjudged *Native Son* and its author just claimants to greatness) conditioned the writing of *Black Boy*. *Native Son*'s reception gave Wright the confidence he needed to deal with a world he viewed as tempting, fragmented, and alienating; in *Black Boy*, the intended message is one of transcend-

---

[21] Ralph Ellison, "Richard Wright's Blues," in *Shadow and Act* (New York: Signet, 1966), pp. 89–104.

[22] Dan McCall, *The Example of Richard Wright* (New York: Harcourt, Brace Jovanovich, 1969).

[23] Wright, *Black Boy*, p. 45. Wright's entire statement is parenthetical and occurs at the beginning of Chapter Two.

ence, and in order to drive home its full significance, the author allows monochromatic or unrelieved barrenness to serve as scrim and underpinning for the stage on which his narrator acts out his ascent. The total effect of *Black Boy* is magnificent; we bestow kudos where the autobiographer intends—on the hard-earned rise of Richard Wright to his position as author.

Once again, however, we see the same type of paradox that confronts the reader of "How 'Bigger' Was Born." It must be kept in mind that a transcendent Richard Wright—an author who had repeatedly employed the communality, modes of adaptation, and intraracial hostility of black culture as subjects for his fiction—tells the reader of a sterile culture that can scarcely be expected to produce such an author. In short, Wright's position as some readers view it (those observers who perceive him objectively as a writer whose genius was brought to maturity by the group in which he had his genesis) is a tribute to the vitality and creativity of black culture. His position as he perceived it, however, was an altogether different thing, since he regarded himself as both subject and object. And in considering his subject for *Black Boy*, he was somewhat myopic: he was unable to see his developed self as sensitive readers can. His pejorative comments on black American culture, therefore, are balanced by the reader's understanding of what Wright sought to achieve, and the fact that he chose to write what Roy Pascal [24] designates "the story of a calling" implies an affirmation of black American culture's ability to produce outstanding authors. A knowledge of black culture offers one key to understanding Wright's life and works.

The impulses from Wright's culture conditioned his propensity for other realms of experience and influenced his definition of an authorial relationship to them. Bigger Thomas's final stance in *Native Son*, for example, is as existential as Cross Damon's primary stance in *The Outsider*. Yet it was not Wright's contact with Jean Paul Sartre and Simone de Beauvoir that shaped his existential view. The fundamental conditions of black life in America led him to see that a priori moral values could scarcely be operating in the great scheme of events; the quest for value in *Native Son* and *The Outsider*, therefore, does not extend beyond the choices of an individual man with his mind "set on freedom." In the same vein, Wright states in *Black Boy* that his choice of literary

[24] Roy Pascal, *Design and Truth in Autobiography* (Cambridge, Mass.: Harvard University Press, 1960).

mode was not the result of over-intellectualization or excessive brooding on white Western culture: "All my life had shaped me for the realism, the naturalism of the modern novel, and I could not read enough of them" (p. 274). Black life in America, which is both existential and communal, was thoroughly naturalistic for Richard Wright.

Though he sought means to order the seeming chaos of the black situation, that chaos and the means, values, and strategies that his fellow black Americans used to cope with it were always integral parts of his outlook. In his first novel, he gazed steadily on the face of chaos and created a successful and enduring work, and if one holds *Native Son* alone in evidence, one must agree with Hugh Gloster[25] that ". . . [Wright] above all other American novelists, is the sensitive painter and perspicacious spokesman of the inarticulate black millions of this country." In "Blueprint for Negro Literature" (published in *New Challenge*, 1937), Wright himself wrote:

> It was, however, in a folklore moulded out of rigorous and inhuman conditions of life that the Negro achieved his most indigenous expression. Blues, spirituals, and folk tales recounted from mouth to mouth, the whispered words of a black mother to her black daughter on the ways of men, the confidential wisdom of a black father to his back son, the swapping of sex experiences on street corners from boy to boy in the deepest vernacular, work songs sung under blazing suns, all these formed the channels through which the racial wisdom flowed.[26]

In recording his experiences as an orderly in a Chicago hospital in 1931, Wright tells of assisting as doctors sedated experimental dogs, stuck scalpels down their throats, and slit their vocal cords so that they would not disturb the patients. The awakened dogs, who lifted their eyes to the ceiling and attempted to cry, became for Wright symbols of silent suffering. Wright's statement in "Blueprint" merges with his experiences in the Chicago hospital, to give a very special impact to Gloster's assessment of his achievement in *Native Son*. Richard Wright moved beyond inarticulateness— beyond silent suffering; yet when he created it was in the tone

[25] Hugh Gloster, *Negro Voices in American Fiction* (Chapel Hill, N.C.: University of North Carolina Press, 1948).

[26] Richard Wright, "Blueprint for Negro Literature," *Amistad* 2 (New York: Random House, 1971), p. 6. *Amistad* is a journal of black history and culture. Included in the second issue is a revised and expanded version of Wright's "Blueprint."

and from the perspective of the "inarticulate" black folk of America. The "racial wisdom" of an accomplished cultural heritage flows through *Native Son,* one of the most dynamic novels in the black American literary tradition.

Richard Wright's work has received so much critical attention during the last thirty years that one almost hesitates to attempt a collection of the most outstanding criticism on even a single novel. I am sure that the works that follow represent only a small portion of the worthwhile and valuable critical comments that have been made about *Native Son.* I am indebted to a number of people for their help in assembling this volume; though I am fully aware that the value judgments reflected by my introductory comments and my selection of materials remain my own responsibility. I would like to thank Ernest Kaiser for his help in securing materials and for his suggestions about bibliography. The staff members of the Schomburg and the Beinecke libraries were cooperative at every stage of my work. My typist, Miss Frances Lacky, provided valuable editorial suggestions, and the Center for Advanced Studies. at the University of Virginia enabled me to travel in search of materials. Professor Raymond Nelson of the University of Virginia spent a number of hours discussing my ideas and the design of the book, and my research assistant, Mr. Tom Bush, worked diligently and faithfully. Finally, my wife gave both the encouragement and the patience needed for the completion of my task.

Houston A. Baker, Jr.

How "Bigger" Was Born

by Richard Wright

I am not so pretentious as to imagine that it is possible for me to account completely for my own book, *Native Son*. But I am going to try to account for as much of it as I can, the sources of it, the material that went into it, and my own years' long changing attitude toward that material.

In a fundamental sense, an imaginative novel represents the merging of two extremes; it is an intensely intimate expression on the part of a consciousness couched in terms of the most objective and commonly known events. It is at once something private and public by its very nature and texture. Confounding the author who is trying to lay his cards on the table is the dogging knowledge that his imagination is a kind of community medium of exchange: what he has read, felt, thought, seen, and remembered is translated into extensions as impersonal as a worn dollar bill.

The more closely the author thinks of why he wrote, the more he comes to regard his imagination as a kind of self-generating cement which glued his facts together, and his emotions as a kind of dark and obscure designer of those facts. Always there is something that is just beyond the tip of the tongue that could explain it all. Usually, he ends up by discussing something far afield, an act which incites skepticism and suspicion in those anxious for a straight-out explanation.

Yet the author is eager to explain. But the moment he makes the attempt his words falter, for he is confronted and defied by the inexplicable array of his own emotions. Emotions are subjec-

"How 'Bigger' Was Born" from Native Son, *Perennial edition, by Richard Wright (New York: Harper & Row, Publishers, Inc., 1966) pp. 1–39. Copyright © 1940 by Richard Wright; renewed 1968 by Ellen Wright. Reprinted by permission of Harper & Row, Publishers, Inc. and Jonathan Cape Ltd.*

Parts of this article originally appeared in the Saturday Review of Literature, *XXII (June 1, 1940).*

The ellipses are Wright's.

tive and he can communicate them only when he clothes them in objective guise; and how can he ever be so arrogant as to know when he is dressing up the right emotion in the right Sunday suit? He is always left with the uneasy notion that maybe *any* objective drapery is as good as *any* other for any emotion.

And the moment he does dress up an emotion, his mind is confronted with the riddle of that "dressed up" emotion, and he is left peering with eager dismay back into the dim reaches of his own incommunicable life. Reluctantly, he comes to the conclusion that to account for his book is to account for his life, and he knows that that is impossible. Yet, some curious, wayward motive urges him to supply the answer, for there is the feeling that his dignity as a living being is challenged by something within him that is not understood.

So, at the outset, I say frankly that there are phases of *Native Son* which I shall make no attempt to account for. There are meanings in my book of which I was not aware until they literally spilled out upon the paper. I shall sketch the outline of how I *consciously* came into possession of the materials that went into *Native Son,* but there will be many things I shall omit, not because I want to, but simply because I don't know them.

The birth of Bigger Thomas goes back to my childhood, and there was not just one Bigger, but many of them, more than I could count and more than you suspect. But let me start with the first Bigger, whom I shall call Bigger No. 1.

When I was a bareheaded, barefoot kid in Jackson, Mississippi, there was a boy who terrorized me and all of the boys I played with. If we were playing games, he would saunter up and snatch from us our balls, bats, spinning tops, and marbles. We would stand around pouting, sniffling, trying to keep back our tears, begging for our playthings. But Bigger would refuse. We never demanded that he give them back; we were afraid, and Bigger was bad. We had seen him clout boys when he was angry and we did not want to run that risk. We never recovered our toys unless we flattered him and made him feel that he was superior to us. Then, perhaps, if he felt like it, he condescended, threw them at us and then gave each of us a swift kick in the bargain, just to make us feel his utter contempt.

That was the way Bigger No. 1 lived. His life was a continuous challenge to others. At all times he *took* his way, right or wrong, and those who contradicted him had him to fight. And never was he happier than when he had someone cornered and at his mercy; it seemed that the deepest meaning of his squalid life was in him at such times.

I don't know what the fate of Bigger No. 1 was. His swaggering personality is swallowed up somewhere in the amnesia of my childhood. But I suspect that his end was violent. Anyway, he left a marked impression upon me; maybe it was because I longed secretly to be like him and was afraid. I don't know.

If I had known only one Bigger I would not have written *Native Son*. Let me call the next one Bigger No. 2; he was about seventeen and tougher than the first Bigger. Since I, too, had grown older, I was a little less afraid of him. And the hardness of this Bigger No. 2 was not directed toward me or the other Negroes, but toward the whites who ruled the South. He bought clothes and food on credit and would not pay for them. He lived in the dingy shacks of the white landlords and refused to pay rent. Of course, he had no money, but neither did we. We did without the necessities of life and starved ourselves, but he never would. When we asked him why he acted as he did, he would tell us (as though we were little children in a kindergarten) that the white folks had everything and he had nothing. Further, he would tell us that we were fools not to get what we wanted while we were alive in this world. We would listen and silently agree. We longed to believe and act as he did, but we were afraid. We were Southern Negroes and we were hungry and we wanted to live, but we were more willing to tighten our belts than risk conflict. Bigger No. 2 wanted to live and he did; he was in prison the last time I heard from him.

There was Bigger No. 3, whom the white folks called a "bad nigger." He carried his life in his hands in a literal fashion. I once worked as a ticket-taker in a Negro movie house (all movie houses in Dixie are Jim Crow; there are movies for whites and movies for blacks), and many times Bigger No. 3 came to the door and gave my arm a hard pinch and walked into the theater. Resentfully and silently, I'd nurse my bruised arm. Presently, the proprietor would come over and ask how things were going. I'd point into the darkened theater and say: "Bigger's in there." "Did he pay?" the proprietor would ask. "No, sir," I'd answer. The proprietor would pull down the corners of his lips and speak through his teeth: "We'll kill that goddamn nigger one of these days." And the episode would end right there. But later on Bigger No. 3 was killed during the days of Prohibition: while delivering liquor to a customer he was shot through the back by a white cop.

And then there was Bigger No. 4, whose only law was death. The Jim Crow laws of the South were not for him. But as he laughed and cursed and broke them, he knew that some day he'd have to pay for his freedom. His rebellious spirit made him violate all the taboos and consequently he always oscillated between moods of intense elation and depression. He was never happier than when he had outwitted some foolish custom, and he was never more melancholy than when brooding over the impossibility of his ever being free. He had no job, for he regarded digging ditches for fifty cents a day as slavery. "I can't live on that," he would say. Ofttimes I'd find him reading a book; he would stop and in a joking, wistful, and cynical manner ape the antics of the white folks. Generally, he'd end his mimicry in a depressed state and say: "The white folks won't let us do nothing." Bigger No. 4 was sent to the asylum for the insane.

Then there was Bigger No. 5, who always rode the Jim Crow streetcars without paying and sat wherever he pleased. I remember one morning his getting into a streetcar (all streetcars in Dixie are divided into two sections: one section is for whites and is labeled —FOR WHITES; the other section is for Negroes and is labeled —FOR COLORED) and sitting in the white section. The conductor went to him and said: "Come on, nigger. Move over where you belong. Can't you read?" Bigger answered: "Naw, I can't read." The conductor flared up: "Get out of that seat!" Bigger took out his knife, opened it, held it nonchalantly in his hand, and replied: "Make me." The conductor turned red, blinked, clenched his fists, and walked away, stammering: "The goddamn scum of the earth!" A small angry conference of white men took place in the front of the car and the Negroes sitting in the Jim Crow section overheard: "That's that Bigger Thomas nigger and you'd better leave 'im alone." The Negroes experienced an intense flash of pride and the streetcar moved on its journey without incident. I don't know what happened to Bigger No. 5. But I can guess.

The Bigger Thomases were the only Negroes I know of who consistently violated the Jim Crow laws of the South and got away with it, at least for a sweet brief spell. Eventually, the whites who restricted their lives made them pay a terrible price. They were shot, hanged, maimed, lynched, and generally hounded until they were either dead or their spirits broken.

There were many variations to this behavioristic pattern. Later on I encountered other Bigger Thomases who did not react to the locked-in Black Belts with this same extremity and violence. But before I use Bigger Thomas as a springboard for the examination of milder types, I'd better indicate more precisely the nature of the environment that produced these men, or the reader will be left with the impression that they were essentially and organically bad.

In Dixie there are two worlds, the white world and the black world, and they are physically separated. There are white schools and black schools, white churches and black churches, white businesses and black businesses, white graveyards and black graveyards, and, for all I know, a white God and a black God. . . .

This separation was accomplished after the Civil War by the terror of the Ku Klux Klan, which swept the newly freed Negro through arson, pillage, and death out of the United States Senate, the House of Representatives, the many state legislatures, and out of the public, social, and economic life of the South. The motive for this assault was simple and urgent. The imperialistic tug of history had torn the Negro from his African home and had placed him ironically upon the most fertile plantation areas of the South; and, when the Negro was freed, he outnumbered the whites in many of these fertile areas. Hence, a fierce and bitter struggle took place to keep the ballot from the Negro, for had he had a chance to vote, he would have automatically controlled the richest lands of the South and with them the social, political, and economic destiny of a third of the Republic. Though the South is politically a part of America, the problem that faced her was peculiar and the struggle between the whites and the blacks after the Civil War was in essence a struggle for power, ranging over thirteen states and involving the lives of tens of millions of people.

But keeping the ballot from the Negro was not enough to hold him in check; disfranchisement had to be supplemented by a whole panoply of rules, taboos, and penalties designed not only to insure peace (complete submission), but to guarantee that no real threat would ever arise. Had the Negro lived upon a common territory, separate from the bulk of the white population, this program of oppression might not have assumed such a brutal and violent form. But this war took place between people who were neighbors, whose homes adjoined, whose farms had common boundaries. Guns and disfranchisement, therefore, were not enough to make the black neighbor keep his distance. The white neighbor decided to limit the amount of education his black neighbor could receive; decided to keep him off the police force and out of the local national guards; to segregate him residentially; to Jim Crow him in public places; to restrict his participation in the professions and jobs; and to build up a vast, dense ideology of racial superiority that would justify any act of violence taken against him to defend white dominance; and further, to condition him to hope for little and to receive that little without rebelling.

But, because the blacks were so *close* to the very civilization which sought to keep them out, because they could not *help* but react in some way to its incentives and prizes, and because the very tissue of their consciousness received its tone and timbre from the strivings of that dominant civilization, oppression spawned among them a myriad variety of reactions, reaching from outright blind rebellion to a sweet, otherworldly submissiveness.

In the main, this delicately balanced state of affairs has not greatly altered since the Civil War, save in those parts of the South which have been industrialized or urbanized. So volatile and tense are these relations that if a Negro rebels against rule and taboo, he is lynched and the reason for the lynching is usually called "rape," that catchword which has garnered such vile connotations that it can raise a mob anywhere in the South pretty quickly, even today.

Now for the variations in the Bigger Thomas pattern. Some of the Negroes living under these conditions got religion, felt that Jesus would redeem the void of living, felt that the more bitter life was in the present the happier it would be in the hereafter. Others, clinging still to that brief glimpse of post-Civil War freedom, employed a thousand ruses and stratagems of struggle to win their rights. Still others projected their hurts and longings into more naïve and mundane forms—blues, jazz, swing—and, without intellectual guidance, tried to build up a compensatory nourishment for themselves. Many labored under hot suns and then killed the restless ache with alcohol. Then there were those who strove for an education, and when they got it, enjoyed the financial fruits of it in the style of their bourgeois oppressors. Usually they went hand in hand with the powerful whites and helped to keep their groaning brothers in line, for that was the safest course of action. Those who did this called themselves "leaders." To give you an idea of how completely these "leaders" worked with those who oppressed, I can tell you that I lived the first seventeen years of my life in the South without so much as hearing of or seeing one act of rebellion from *any* Negro, save the Bigger Thomases.

But why did Bigger revolt? No explanation based upon a hard and fast rule of conduct can be given. But there were always two factors psychologically dominant in his personality. First, through some quirk of circumstance, he had become estranged from the religion and the folk culture of his race. Second, he was trying to react to and answer the call of the dominant civilization whose glitter came to him through the newspapers, magazines, radios, movies, and the mere imposing sight and sound of daily American life. In many respects his emergence as a distinct type was inevitable.

As I grew older, I became familiar with the Bigger Thomas conditioning and its numerous shadings no matter where I saw it in Negro life. It was not, as I have already said, as blatant or extreme as in the originals; but it was there, nevertheless, like an undeveloped negative.

Sometimes, in areas far removed from Mississippi, I'd hear a Negro say: "I wish I didn't have to live this way. I feel like I want to burst." Then the anger would pass; he would go back to his job and try to eke out a few pennies to support his wife and children.

Sometimes I'd hear a Negro say: "God, I wish I had a flag and a country of my own." But that mood would soon vanish and he would go his way placidly enough.

Sometimes I'd hear a Negro ex-soldier say: "What in hell did I fight in the war for? They segregated me even when I was offering my life for my country." But he, too, like the others, would soon forget, would become caught up in the tense grind of struggling for bread.

I've even heard Negroes, in moments of anger and bitterness, praise what Japan is doing in China, not because they believed in oppression (being objects of oppression themselves), but because they would suddenly sense how empty their lives were when looking at the dark faces of Japanese generals in the rotogravure supplements of the Sunday newspapers. They would dream of what it would be like to live in a country where they could forget their color and play a responsible role in the vital processes of the nation's life.

I've even heard Negroes say that maybe Hitler and Mussolini are

all right; that maybe Stalin is all right. They did not say this out
of any intellectual comprehension of the forces at work in the
world, but because they felt that these men "did things," a phrase
which is charged with more meaning than the mere words imply.
There was in the back of their minds, when they said this, a wild
and intense longing (wild and intense because it was suppressed!)
to belong, to be identified, to feel that they were alive as other
people were, to be caught up forgetfully and exultingly in the
swing of events, to feel the clean, deep, organic satisfaction of doing
a job in common with others.

It was not until I went to live in Chicago that I first thought
seriously of writing of Bigger Thomas. Two items of my experience
combined to make me aware of Bigger as a meaningful and prophetic symbol. First, being free of the daily pressure of the Dixie
environment, I was able to come into possession of my own feelings.
Second, my contact with the labor movement and its ideology made
me see Bigger clearly and feel what he meant.

I made the discovery that Bigger Thomas was not black all the
time; he was white, too, and there were literally millions of him,
everywhere. The extension of my sense of the personality of Bigger
was the pivot of my life; it altered the complexion of my existence.
I became conscious, at first dimly, and then later on with increasing
clarity and conviction, of a vast, muddied pool of human life in
America. It was as though I had put on a pair of spectacles whose
power was that of an x-ray enabling me to see deeper into the lives
of men. Whenever I picked up a newspaper, I'd no longer feel that
I was reading of the doings of whites alone (Negroes are rarely
mentioned in the press unless they've committed some crime!), but
of a complex struggle for life going on in my country, a struggle
in which I was involved. I sensed, too, that the Southern scheme
of oppression was but an appendage of a far vaster and in many
respects more ruthless and impersonal commodity-profit machine.

Trade-union struggles and issues began to grow meaningful to
me. The flow of goods across the seas, buoying and depressing the
wages of men, held a fascination. The pronouncements of foreign
governments, their policies, plans, and acts were calculated and
weighed in relation to the lives of people about me. I was literally
overwhelmed when, in reading the works of Russian revolutionists,
I came across descriptions of the "holiday energies of the masses,"
"the locomotives of history," "the conditions prerequisite for revolution," and so forth. I approached all of these new revelations in

the light of Bigger Thomas, his hopes, fears, and despairs; and I
began to feel far-flung kinships, and sense, with fright and abash-
ment, the possibilities of *alliances* between the American Negro and
other people possessing a kindred consciousness.

As my mind extended in this general and abstract manner, it was
fed with even more vivid and concrete examples of the lives of
Bigger Thomas. The urban environment of Chicago, affording a
more stimulating life, made the Negro Bigger Thomases react more
violently than even in the South. More than ever I began to see
and understand the environmental factors which made for this
extreme conduct. It was not that Chicago segregated Negroes more
than the South, but that Chicago had more to offer, that Chicago's
physical aspect—noisy, crowded, filled with the sense of power and
fulfillment—did so much more to dazzle the mind with a taunting
sense of possible achievement that the segregation it did impose
brought forth from Bigger a reaction more obstreperous than in the
South.

So the concrete picture and the abstract linkages of relationships
fed each other, each making the other more meaningful and affording my emotions an opportunity to react to them with success and
understanding. The process was like a swinging pendulum, each to
and fro motion throwing up its tiny bit of meaning and significance,
each stroke helping to develop the dim negative which had been
implanted in my mind in the South.

During this period the shadings and nuances which were filling
in Bigger's picture came, not so much from Negro life, as from the
lives of whites I met and grew to know. I began to sense that they
had their own kind of Bigger Thomas behavioristic pattern which
grew out of a more subtle and broader frustration. The waves of
recurring crime, the silly fads and crazes, the quicksilver changes in
public taste, the hysteria and fears—all of these had long been
mysteries to me. But now I looked back of them and felt the pinch
and pressure of the environment that gave them their pitch and
peculiar kind of being. I began to feel with my mind the inner
tensions of the people I met. I don't mean to say that I think
that environment *makes* consciousness (I suppose God makes that,
if there is a God), but I do say that I felt and still feel that the environment supplies the instrumentalities through which the organism expresses itself, and if that environment is warped or tranquil,
the mode and manner of behavior will be affected toward deadlock-
ing tensions or orderly fulfillment and satisfaction.

Let me give examples of how I began to develop the dim negative
of Bigger. I met white writers who talked of their responses, who
told me how whites reacted to this lurid American scene. And, as
they talked, I'd translate what they said in terms of Bigger's life.
But what was more important still, I read their novels. Here, for
the first time, I found ways and techniques of gauging meaningfully
the effects of American civilization upon the personalities of people.
I took these techniques, these ways of seeing and feeling, and twisted
them, bent them, adapted them, until they became *my* ways of
apprehending the locked-in life of the Black Belt areas. This association with white writers was the life preserver of my hope to
depict Negro life in fiction, for my race possessed no fictional works
dealing with such problems, had no background in such sharp and
critical testing of experience, no novels that went with a deep and
fearless will down to the dark roots of life.

Here are examples of how I culled information relating to Bigger
from my reading:

There is in me a memory of reading an interesting pamphlet telling of the friendship of Gorky and Lenin in exile. The booklet told
of how Lenin and Gorky were walking down a London street. Lenin
turned to Gorky and, pointing, said: "Here is *their* Big Ben."
"There is *their* Westminster Abbey." "There is *their* library." And
at once, while reading that passage, my mind stopped, teased, challenged with the effort to remember, to associate widely disparate
but meaningful experiences in my life. For a moment nothing would
come, but I remained convinced that I had heard the meaning of
those words sometime, somewhere before. Then, with a sudden
glow of satisfaction of having gained a little more knowledge about
the world in which I lived, I'd end up by saying: "That's Bigger.
That's the Bigger Thomas reaction."

In both instances the deep sense of exclusion was identical. The
feeling of looking at things with a painful and unwarrantable naked-
ness was an experience, I learned, that transcended national and
racial boundaries. It was this intolerable sense of feeling and understanding so much, and yet living on a plane of social reality where
the look of a world which one did not make or own struck one with
a blinding objectivity and tangibility, that made me grasp the revolutionary impulse in my life and the lives of those about me and
far away.

I remember reading a passage in a book dealing with old Russia
which said: "We must be ready to make endless sacrifices if we are

to be able to overthrow the Czar." And again I'd say to myself: "I've heard that somewhere, sometime before." And again I'd hear Bigger Thomas, far away and long ago, telling some white man who was trying to impose upon him: "I'll kill you and go to hell and pay for it." While living in America I heard from far away Russia the bitter accents of tragic calculation of how much human life and suffering it would cost a man to live as a man in a world that denied him the right to live with dignity. Actions and feelings of men ten thousand miles from home helped me to understand the moods and impulses of those walking the streets of Chicago and Dixie.

I am not saying that I heard any talk of revolution in the South when I was a kid there. But I did hear the lispings, the whispers, the mutters which some day, under one stimulus or another, will surely grow into open revolt unless the conditions which produce Bigger Thomases are changed.

In 1932 another source of information was dramatically opened up to me and I saw data of a surprising nature that helped to clarify the personality of Bigger. From the moment that Hitler took power in Germany and began to oppress the Jews, I tried to keep track of what was happening. And on innumerable occasions I was startled to detect, either from the side of the Fascists or from the side of the oppressed, reactions, moods, phrases, attitudes that reminded me strongly of Bigger, that helped to bring out more clearly the shadowy outlines of the negative that lay in the back of my mind.

I read every account of the Fascist movement in Germany I could lay my hands on, and from page to page I encountered and recognized familiar emotional patterns. What struck me with particular force was the Nazi preoccupation with the construction of a society in which there would exist among all people (*German* people, of course!) *one* solidarity of ideals, *one* continuous circulation of fundamental beliefs, notions, and assumptions. I am not now speaking of the popular idea of regimenting people's thought; I'm speaking of the implicit, almost unconscious, or pre-conscious, assumptions and ideals upon which whole nations and races act and live. And while reading these Nazi pages I'd be reminded of the Negro preacher in the South telling of a life beyond this world, a life in which the color of men's skins would not matter, a life in which each man would know what was deep down in the hearts of his fellow man. And I could hear Bigger Thomas standing on a street corner in America expressing his agonizing doubts and chronic suspicions, thus: "I ain't going to trust nobody. Everything is a racket and everybody is out to get what he can for himself. Maybe if we had a true leader, we could do something." And I'd know that I was still on the track of learning about Bigger, still in the midst of the modern struggle for solidarity among men.

When the Nazis spoke of the necessity of a highly ritualized and symbolized life, I could hear Bigger Thomas on Chicago's South Side saying: "Man, what we need is a leader like Marcus Garvey. We need a nation, a flag, an army of our own. We colored folks ought to organize into groups and have generals, captains, lieutenants, and so forth. We ought to take Africa and have a national home." I'd know, while listening to these childish words, that a white man would smile derisively at them. But I could not smile, for I knew the truth of those simple words from the facts of my own life. The deep hunger in those childish ideas was like a flash of lightning illuminating the whole dark inner landscape of Bigger's mind. Those words told me that the civilization which had given birth to Bigger contained no spiritual sustenance, had created no culture which could hold and claim his allegiance and faith, had sensitized him and had left him stranded, a free agent to roam the streets of our cities, a hot and whirling vortex of undisciplined and unchannelized impulses. The results of these observations made me feel more than ever estranged from the civilization in which I lived, and more than ever resolved toward the task of creating with words a scheme of images and symbols whose direction could enlist the sympathies, loyalties, and yearnings of the millions of Bigger Thomases in every land and race. . . .

But more than anything else, as a writer, I was fascinated by the similarity of the emotional tensions of Bigger in America and Bigger in Nazi Germany and Bigger in old Russia. All Bigger Thomases, white and black, felt tense, afraid, nervous, hysterical, and restless. From far away Nazi Germany and old Russia had come to me items of knowledge that told me that certain modern experiences were creating types of personalities whose existence ignored racial and national lines of demarcation, that these personalities carried with them a more universal drama-element than anything I'd ever encountered before; that these personalities were mainly imposed upon men and women living in a world whose fundamental assumptions could no longer be taken for granted: a world ridden with national and class strife: a world whose metaphysical meanings had vanished; a world in which God no longer existed as a daily focal point of men's lives; a world in which men could no longer retain their faith in an ultimate hereafter. It was a highly geared world whose nature was conflict and action, a world whose limited area and vision imperiously urged men to satisfy their organisms, a world that existed on a plane of animal sensation alone.

It was a world in which millions of men lived and behaved like drunkards, taking a stiff drink of hard life to lift them up for a thrilling moment, to give them a quivering sense of wild exultation and fulfillment that soon faded and let them down. Eagerly they took another drink, wanting to avoid the dull, flat look of things, then still another, this time stronger, and then they felt that their lives had meaning. Speaking figuratively, they were soon chronic alcoholics, men who lived by violence, through extreme action and sensation, through drowning daily in a perpetual nervous agitation.

From these items I drew my first political conclusions about Bigger: I felt that Bigger, an American product, a native son of this land, carried within him the potentialities of either Communism or Fascism. I don't mean to say that the Negro boy I depicted in *Native Son* is either a Communist or a Fascist. He is not either. But he is product of a dislocated society; he is a dispossessed and disinherited man; he is all of this, and he lives amid the greatest possible plenty on earth and he is looking and feeling for a way out. Whether he'll follow some gaudy, hysterical leader who'll promise rashly to fill the void in him, or whether he'll come to an understanding with the millions of his kindred fellow workers under trade-union or revolutionary guidance depends upon the future drift of events in America. But, granting the emotional state, the tensity, the fear, the hate, the impatience, the sense of exclusion, the ache for violent action, the emotional and cultural hunger, Bigger Thomas, conditioned as organism is, will not become an ardent, or even a lukewarm, supporter of the *status quo.*

The difference between Bigger's tensity and the German variety is that Bigger's, due to America's educational restrictions on the bulk of her Negro population, is in a nascent state, not yet articulate. And the difference between Bigger's longing for self-identification and the Russian principle of self-determination is that Bigger's, due to the effects of American oppression, which has not allowed for the forming of deep ideas of solidarity among Negroes, is still in a state of individual anger and hatred. Here, I felt, was *drama!* Who will be the first to touch off these Bigger Thomases in America, white and black?

For a long time I toyed with the idea of writing a novel in which a Negro Bigger Thomas would loom as a symbolic figure of American life, a figure who would hold within him the prophecy of our future. I felt strongly that he held within him, in a measure which perhaps no other contemporary type did, the outlines of action and feeling which we would encounter on a vast scale in the days to come. Just as one sees when one walks into a medical research laboratory jars of alcohol containing abnormally large or distorted portions of the human body, just so did I see and feel that the conditions of life under which Negroes are forced to live in America contain the embryonic emotional prefigurations of how a large part of the body politic would react under stress.

So, with this much knowledge of myself and the world gained and known, why should I not try to work out on paper the problem of what will happen to Bigger? Why should I not, like a scientist in a laboratory, use my imagination and invent test-tube situations, place Bigger in them, and, following the guidance of my own hopes and fears, what I had learned and remembered, work out in fictional form an emotional statement and resolution of this problem?

But several things militated against my starting to work. Like Bigger himself, I felt a mental censor—product of the fears which a Negro feels from living in America—standing over me, draped in white, warning me not to write. This censor's warnings were translated into my own thought processes thus: "What will white people think if I draw the picture of such a Negro boy? Will they not at once say: 'See, didn't we tell you all along that niggers are like that? Now, look, one of their own kind has come along and drawn the picture for us!' " I felt that if I drew the picture of Bigger truthfully, there would be many reactionary whites who would try to make of him something I did not intend. And yet, and this was what made it difficult, I knew that I could not write of Bigger convincingly if I did not depict him as he *was:* that is, resentful toward whites, sullen, angry, ignorant, emotionally unstable, depressed and unaccountably elated at times, and unable even, because of his own lack of inner organization which American oppression has fostered in him, to unite with the members of his own race. And would not whites misread Bigger and, doubting his authenticity, say: "This man is preaching hate against the whole white race"?

The more I thought of it the more I became convinced that if I did not write of Bigger as I saw and felt him, if I did not try to make him a living personality and at the same time a symbol of all the larger things I felt and saw in him, I'd be reacting as Bigger himself reacted: that is, I'd be acting out of *fear* if I let what I thought whites would say constrict and paralyze me.

As I contemplated Bigger and what he meant, I said to myself: "I must write this novel, not only for others to read, but to free *myself* of this sense of shame and fear." In fact, the novel, as time passed, grew upon me to the extent that it became a necessity to write it; the writing of it turned into a way of living for me.

Another thought kept me from writing. What would my own white and black comrades in the Communist party say? This thought was the most bewildering of all. Politics is a hard and narrow game; its policies represent the aggregate desires and aspirations of millions of people. Its goals are rigid and simply drawn, and the minds of the majority of politicians are set, congealed in terms of daily tactical maneuvers. How could I create such complex and wide schemes of associational thought and feeling, such filigreed webs of dreams and politics, without being mistaken for a "smuggler of reaction," "an ideological confusionist," or "an individualistic and dangerous element"? Though my heart is with the collectivist and proletarian ideal, I solved this problem by assuring myself that honest politics and honest feeling in imaginative representation ought to be able to meet on common healthy ground without fear, suspicion, and quarreling. Further, and more importantly, I steeled myself by coming to the conclusion that whether politicians accepted or rejected Bigger did not really matter; my task, as I felt it, was to free myself of this burden of impressions and feelings, recast them into the image of Bigger and make him *true*. Lastly, I felt that a right more immediately deeper than that of politics or race was at stake; that is, a *human* right, the right of a man to think and feel honestly. And especially did this personal and human right bear hard upon me, for temperamentally I am inclined to satisfy the claims of my own ideals rather than the expectations of others. It was this obscure need that had pulled me into the labor movement in the beginning and by exercising it I was but fulfilling what I felt to be the laws of my own growth.

There was another constricting thought that kept me from work. It deals with my own race. I asked myself: "What will Negro doctors, lawyers, dentists, bankers, school teachers, social workers and business men, think of me if I draw such a picture of Bigger?"

I knew from long and painful experience that the Negro middle and professional classes were the people of my own race who were more than others ashamed of Bigger and what he meant. Having narrowly escaped the Bigger Thomas reaction pattern themselves —indeed, still retaining traces of it within the confines of their own timid personalities—they would not relish being publicly reminded of the lowly, shameful depths of life above which they enjoyed their bourgeois lives. Never did they want people, especially *white* people, to think that their lives were so much touched by anything so dark and brutal as Bigger.

Their attitude toward life and art can be summed up in a single paragraph: "But, Mr. Wright, there are so many of us who are *not* like Bigger? Why don't you portray in your fiction the *best* traits of our race, something that will show the white people what we have done in *spite* of oppression? Don't represent anger and bitterness. Smile when a white person comes to you. Never let him feel that you are so small that what he has done to crush you has made you hate him! Oh, above all, save your *pride!*"

But Bigger won over all these claims; he won because I felt that I was hunting on the trail of more exciting and thrilling game. What Bigger meant had claimed me because I felt with all of my being that he was more important than what any person, white or black, would say or try to make of him, more important than any political analysis designed to explain or deny him, more important, even, than my own sense of fear, shame, and diffidence.

But Bigger was still not down upon paper. For a long time I had been writing of him in my mind, but I had yet to put him into an image, a breathing symbol draped out in the guise of the only form of life my native land had allowed me to know intimately, that is, the ghetto life of the American Negro. But the basic reason for my hesitancy was that another and far more complex problem had risen to plague me. Bigger, as I saw and felt him, was a snarl of many realities; he had in him many levels of life.

First, there was his personal and private life, that intimate existence that is so difficult to snare and nail down in fiction, that elusive core of being, that individual data of consciousness which in every man and woman is like that in no other. I had to deal with Bigger's dreams, his fleeting, momentary sensations, his yearning, visions, his deep emotional responses.

Then I was confronted with that part of him that was dual in aspect, dim, wavering, that part of him which is so much a part of *all* Negroes and *all* whites that I realized that I could put it down upon paper only by feeling out its meaning first within the confines of my own life. Bigger was attracted and repelled by the American scene. He was an American, because he was a native son; but he was also a Negro nationalist in a vague sense because he was not allowed to live as an American. Such was his way of life and mine; neither Bigger nor I resided fully in either camp.

Of this dual aspect of Bigger's social consciousness, I placed the nationalistic side first, not because I agreed with Bigger's wild and intense hatred of white people, but because his hate had placed him, like a wild animal at bay, in a position where he was most symbolic and explainable. In other words, his nationalist complex was for me a concept through which I could grasp more of the total meaning of his life than I could in any other way. I tried to approach Bigger's *snarled* and *confused* nationalist feelings with *conscious* and *informed* ones of my own. Yet, Bigger was not nationalist enough to feel the need of religion or the folk culture of his own people. What made Bigger's social consciousness most complex was the fact that he was hovering unwanted between two worlds—between powerful America and his own stunted place in life—and I took upon myself the task of trying to make the reader feel this No Man's Land. The most that I could say of Bigger was that he felt the *need* for a whole life and *acted* out of that need; that was all.

Above and beyond all this, there was that American part of Bigger which is the heritage of us all, that part of him which we get from our seeing and hearing, from school, from the hopes and dreams of our friends; that part of him which the common people of America never talk of but take for granted. Among millions of people the deepest convictions of life are never discussed openly; they are felt, implied, hinted at tacitly and obliquely in their hopes and fears. We live by an idealism that makes us believe that the Constitution is a good document of government, that the Bill of Rights is a good legal and humane principle to safeguard our civil liberties, that every man and woman should have the opportunity to realize himself, to seek his own individual fate and goal, his own peculiar and untranslatable destiny. I don't say that Bigger knew this in the terms in which I'm speaking of it; I don't say that any such thought ever entered his head. His emotional and intellectual life was never that articulate. But he knew it emotionally, intuitively, for his emotions and his desires were developed, and he caught it, as most of us do, from the mental and emotional climate of our time. Bigger had all of this in him, dammed up, buried, implied, and I had to develop it in fictional form.

There was still another level of Bigger's life that I felt bound to account for and render, a level as elusive to discuss as it was to grasp in writing. Here again, I had to fall back upon my own feelings as a guide, for Bigger did not offer in his life any articulate verbal explanations. There seems to hover somewhere in that dark part of all our lives, in some more than in others, an objectless, timeless, spaceless element of primal fear and dread, stemming, perhaps, from our birth (depending upon whether one's outlook upon personality is Freudian or non-Freudian!), a fear and dread which exercises an impelling influence upon our lives all out of proportion to its obscurity. And, accompanying this *first fear,* is, for the want of a better name, a reflex urge toward ecstasy, complete submission, and trust. The springs of religion are here, and also the origins of rebellion. And in a boy like Bigger, young, unschooled, whose subjective life was clothed in the tattered rags of American "culture," this primitive fear and ecstasy were naked, exposed, unprotected by religion or a framework of government or a scheme of society whose final faiths would gain his love and trust; unprotected by trade or profession, faith or belief; opened to every trivial blast of daily or hourly circumstance.

There was yet another level of reality in Bigger's life: the impliedly political. I've already mentioned that Bigger had in him impulses which I had felt were present in the vast upheavals of Russia and Germany. Well, somehow, I had to make these political impulses felt by the reader in terms of Bigger's daily actions, keeping in mind as I did so the probable danger of my being branded as a propagandist by those who would not like the subject matter.

Then there was Bigger's relationship with white America, both North and South, which I had to depict, which I had to make known once again, alas; a relationship whose effects are carried by every Negro, like scars, somewhere in his body and mind.

I had also to show what oppression had done to Bigger's relationships with his own people, how it had split him off from them, how it had baffled him; how oppression seems to hinder and stifle in the victim those very qualities of character which are so essential for an effective struggle against the oppressor.

Then there was the fabulous city in which Bigger lived, an

indescribable city, huge, roaring, dirty, noisy, raw, stark, brutal; a city of extremes: torrid summers and sub-zero winters, white people and black people, the English language and strange tongues, foreign born and native born, scabby poverty and gaudy luxury, high idealism and hard cynicism! A city so young that, in thinking of its short history, one's mind, as it travels backward in time, is stopped abruptly by the barren stretches of wind-swept prairie! But a city old enough to have caught within the homes of its long, straight streets the symbols and images of man's age-old destiny, of truths as old as the mountains and seas, of dramas as abiding as the soul of man itself! A city which has become the pivot of the Eastern, Western, Northern, and Southern poles of the nation. But a city whose black smoke clouds shut out the sunshine for seven months of the year; a city in which, on a fine balmy May morning, one can sniff the stench of the stockyards; a city where people have grown so used to gangs and murders and graft that they have honestly forgotten that government can have a pretense of decency!

With all of this thought out, Bigger was still unwritten. Two events, however, came into my life and accelerated the process, made me sit down and actually start work on the typewriter, and just stop the writing of Bigger in my mind as I walked the streets.

The first event was my getting a job in the South Side Boys' Club, an institution which tried to reclaim the thousands of Negro Bigger Thomases from the dives and the alleys of the Black Belt. Here, on a vast scale, I had an opportunity to observe Bigger in all of his moods, actions, haunts. Here I felt for the first time that the rich folk who were paying my wages did not really give a good goddamn about Bigger, that their kindness was prompted at bottom by a selfish motive. They were paying me to distract Bigger with ping-pong, checkers, swimming, marbles, and baseball in order that he might not roam the streets and harm the valuable white property which adjoined the Black Belt. I am not condemning boys' clubs and ping-pong as such; but these little stopgaps were utterly inadequate to fill up the centuries-long chasm of emptiness which American civilization had created in these Biggers. I felt that I was doing a kind of dressed-up police work, and I hated it.

I would work hard with these Biggers, and when it would come time for me to go home I'd say to myself, under my breath so that no one could hear: "Go to it, boys! Prove to the bastards that gave you these games that life is stronger than ping-pong. . . . Show them that full-blooded life is harder and hotter than they suspect, even though that life is draped in a black skin which at heart they despise. . . ."

They did. The police blotters of Chicago are testimony of how *much* they did. That was the only way I could contain myself for doing a job I hated; for a moment I'd allow myself, vicariously, to feel as Bigger felt—not much, just a little, just a *little*—but, still, there it was.

The second event that spurred me to write of Bigger was more personal and subtle. I had written a book of short stories which was published under the title of *Uncle Tom's Children*. When the reviews of that book began to appear, I realized that I had made an awfully naïve mistake. I found that I had written a book which even bankers' daughters could read and weep over and feel good about. I swore to myself that if I ever wrote another book, no one would weep over it; that it would be so hard and deep that they would have to face it without the consolation of tears. It was this that made me get to work in dead earnest.

Now, until this moment I did not stop to think very much about the plot of *Native Son*. The reason I did not is because I was not for one moment ever worried about it. I had spent years learning about Bigger, what had made him, what he meant; so, when the time came for writing, *what had made him and what he meant* constituted my plot. But the far-flung items of his life had to be couched in imaginative terms, terms known and acceptable to a common body of readers, terms which would, in the course of the story, manipulate the deepest held notions and convictions of their lives. That came easy. The moment I began to write, the plot fell out, so to speak. I'm not trying to oversimplify or make the process seem oversubtle. At bottom, what happened is very easy to explain.

Any Negro who has lived in the North or the South knows that times without number he has heard of some Negro boy being picked up on the streets and carted off to jail and charged with "rape." This thing happens so often that to my mind it had become a representative symbol of the Negro's uncertain position in America. Never for a second was I in doubt as to what kind of social reality or dramatic situation I'd put Bigger in, what kind of test-tube life I'd set up to evoke his deepest reactions. Life had made the plot over and over again, to the extent that I knew it by heart. So frequently do these acts recur that when I was halfway through the first draft of *Native Son* a case paralleling Bigger's flared forth in the newspapers of Chicago. (Many of the newspaper items and some of the incidents in *Native Son* are but fictionalized versions of the Robert Nixon case and rewrites of news stories from the *Chicago Tribune*.) Indeed, scarcely was *Native Son* off the press before Supreme Court Justice Hugo L. Black gave the nation a long and vivid account of the American police methods of handling Negro boys.

Let me describe this stereotyped situation: A crime wave is sweeping a city and citizens are clamoring for police action. Squad cars cruise the Black Belt and grab the first Negro boy who seems to be unattached and homeless. He is held for perhaps a week without charge or bail, without the privilege of communicating with anyone, including his own relatives. After a few days this boy "confesses" anything that he is asked to confess, any crime that handily happens to be unsolved and on the calendar. Why does he confess? After the boy has been grilled night and day, hanged up by his thumbs, dangled by his feet out of twenty-story windows, and beaten (in places that leave no scars—cops have found a way to do that), he signs the papers before him, papers which are usually accompanied by a verbal promise to the boy that he will not go to the electric chair. Of course, he ends up by being executed or sentenced for life. If you think I'm telling tall tales, get chummy with some white cop who works in a Black Belt district and ask him for the lowdown.

When a black boy is carted off to jail in such a fashion, it is almost impossible to do anything for him. Even well-disposed Negro lawyers find it difficult to defend him, for the boy will plead guilty one day and then not guilty the next, according to the degree of pressure and persuasion that is brought to bear upon his frightened personality from one side or the other. Even the boy's own family is scared to death; sometimes fear of police intimidation makes them hesitate to acknowledge that the boy is a blood relation of theirs.

Such has been America's attitude toward these boys that if one is picked up and confronted in a police cell with ten white cops, he is intimidated almost to the point of confessing anything. So far removed are these practices from what the average American citizen encounters in his daily life that it takes a huge act of his imagination to believe that it is true; yet, this same average citizen, with his kindness, his American sportsmanship and good will, would probably act with the mob if a self-respecting Negro family moved into his apartment building to escape the Black Belt and its terrors and limitations. . . .

Now, after all of this, when I sat down to the typewriter, I could not work; I could not think of a good opening scene for the book. I had definitely in mind the kind of emotion I wanted to evoke in the reader in that first scene, but I could not think of the type of concrete event that would convey the motif of the entire scheme of the book, that would sound, in varied form, the note that was to be resounded throughout its length, that would introduce to the reader just what kind of an organism Bigger's was and the environment that was bearing hourly upon it. Twenty or thirty times I tried and failed; then I argued that if I could not write the opening scene, I'd start with the scene that followed. I did. The actual writing of the book began with the scene in the pool room.

Now, for the writing. During the years in which I had met all of those Bigger Thomases, those varieties of Bigger Thomases, I had not consciously gathered material to write of them; I had not kept a notebook record of their sayings and doings. Their actions had simply made impressions upon my sensibilities as I lived from day to day, impressions which crystallized and coagulated into clusters and configurations of memory, attitudes, moods, ideas. And these subjective states, in turn, were automatically stored away somewhere in me. I was not even aware of the process. But, excited over the book which I had set myself to write, under the stress of emotion, these things came surging up, tangled, fused, knotted, entertaining me by the sheer variety and potency of their meaning and suggestiveness.

With the whole theme in mind, in an attitude almost akin to prayer, I gave myself up to the story. In an effort to capture some phase of Bigger's life that would not come to me readily, I'd jot down as much of it as I could. Then I'd read it over and over, adding each time a word, a phrase, a sentence until I felt that I had caught all the shadings of reality I felt dimly were there. With each of these rereadings and rewritings it seemed that I'd gather in facts and facets that tried to run away. It was an act of concentration, of trying to hold within one's center of attention all of that bewildering array of facts which science, politics, experience, memory, and imagination were urging upon me. And then, while writing, a new and thrilling relationship would spring up under the drive of emotion, coalescing and telescoping alien facts into a known and felt truth. That was the deep fun of the job: to feel within my body that I was pushing out to new areas of feeling, strange landmarks of emotion, tramping upon foreign soil, compounding new relationships of perceptions, making new and— until that very split second of time!—unheard-of and unfelt effects with words. It had a buoying and tonic impact upon me; my senses would strain and seek for more and more of such relationships, my temperature would rise as I worked. That is writing as I feel it, a kind of significant living.

The first draft of the novel was written in four months, straight through, and ran to some 576 pages. Just as a man rises in the mornings to dig ditches for his bread, so I'd work daily. I'd think of some abstract principle of Bigger's conduct and at once my mind would turn it into some act I'd seen Bigger perform, some act which I hoped would be familiar enough to the American reader to gain his credence. But in the writing of scene after scene I was guided by but one criterion: to tell the truth as I saw it and felt it. That is, to objectify in words some insight derived from my living in the form of action, scene, and dialogue. If a scene seemed improbable to me, I'd not tear it up, but ask myself: "Does it reveal enough of what I feel to stand in spite of its unreality?" If I felt it did, it stood. If I felt that it did not, I ripped it out. The degree of morality in my writing depended upon the degree of felt life and truth I could put down upon the printed page: For example, there is a scene in *Native Son* where Bigger stands in a cell with a Negro preacher, Jan, Max, the State's Attorney, Mr. Dalton, Mrs. Dalton, Bigger's mother, his brother, his sister, Al, Gus, and Jack. While writing that scene, I knew that it was unlikely that so many people would ever be allowed to come into a murderer's cell. But I wanted those people in that cell to elicit a certain important emotional response from Bigger. And so the scene stood. I felt that what I wanted that scene to say to the reader was *more important than its surface reality or plausibility*.

Always, as I wrote, I was both reader and writer, both the conceiver of the action and the appreciator of it. I tried to write so that, in the same instant of time, the objective and subjective aspects of Bigger's life would be caught in a focus of prose. And always I tried to *render, depict,* not merely to tell the story. If a thing was cold, I tried to make the reader *feel* cold, and not just

tell about it. In writing in this fashion, sometimes I'd find it necessary to use a stream of consciousness technique, then rise to an
interior monologue, descend to a direct rendering of a dream state,
then to a matter-of-fact depiction of what Bigger was saying, doing,
and feeling. Then I'd find it impossible to say what I wanted to
say without stepping in and speaking outright on my own; but
when doing this I always made an effort to retain the mood of the
story, explaining everything only in terms of Bigger's life and,
if possible, in the rhythms of Bigger's thought (even though the
words would be mine). Again, at other times, in the guise of the
lawyer's speech and the newspaper items, or in terms of what Bigger
would overhear or see from afar, I'd give what others were saying
and thinking of him. But always, from the start to the finish, it was
Bigger's story, Bigger's fear, Bigger's flight, and Bigger's fate that I
tried to depict. I wrote with the conviction in mind (I don't know
if this is right or wrong; I only know that I'm temperamentally
inclined to feel this way) that the main burden of all serious fiction
consists almost wholly of character-destiny and the items, social,
political, and personal, of that character-destiny.

As I wrote I followed, almost unconsciously, many principles
of the novel which my reading of the novels of other writers had
made me feel were necessary for the building of a well-constructed
book. For the most part the novel is rendered in the present; I
wanted the reader to feel that Bigger's story was happening *now,*
like a play upon the stage or a movie unfolding upon the screen.
Action follows action, as in a prize fight. Wherever possible, I told
of Bigger's life in close-up, slow-motion, giving the feel of the grain
in the passing of time. I had long had the feeling that this was the
best way to "enclose" the reader's mind in a new world, to blot out
all reality except that which I was giving him.

Then again, as much as I could, I restricted the novel to what
Bigger saw and felt, to the limits of his feeling and thoughts, even
when I was conveying *more* than that to the reader. I had the
notion that such a manner of rendering made for a sharper effect,
a more pointed sense of the character, his peculiar type of being
and consciousness. Throughout there is but one point of view:
Bigger's. This, too, I felt, made for a richer illusion of reality.

I kept out of the story as much as possible, for I wanted the
reader to feel that there was nothing between him and Bigger;
that the story was a special *première* given in his own private
theater.

I kept the scenes long, made as much happen within a short space of time as possible; all of which, I felt, made for greater density and richness of effect.

In a like manner I tried to keep a unified sense of background throughout the story; the background would change, of course, but I tried to keep before the eyes of the reader at all times the forces and elements against which Bigger was striving.

And, because I had limited myself to rendering only what Bigger saw and felt, I gave no more reality to the other characters than that which Bigger himself saw.

This, honestly, is all I can account for in the book. If I attempted to account for scenes and characters, to tell why certain scenes were written in certain ways, I'd be stretching facts in order to be pleasantly intelligible. All else in the book came from my feelings reacting upon the material, and any honest reader knows as much about the rest of what is in the book as I do; that is, if, as he reads, he is willing to let his emotions and imagination become as influenced by the materials as I did. As I wrote, for some reason or other, one image, symbol, character, scene, mood, feeling evoked its opposite, its parallel, its complimentary, and its ironic counterpart. Why? I don't know. My emotions and imagination just like to work that way. One can account for just so much of life, and then no more. At least, not yet.

With the first draft down, I found that I could not end the book satisfactorily. In the first draft I had Bigger going smack to the electric chair; but I felt that two murders were enough for one novel. I cut the final scene and went back to worry about the beginning. I had no luck. The book was one-half finished, with the opening and closing scenes unwritten. Then, one night, in desperation—I hope that I'm not disclosing the hidden secrets of my craft!—I sneaked out and got a bottle. With the help of it, I began to remember many things which I could not remember before. One of them was that Chicago was overrun with rats. I recalled that I'd seen many rats on the streets, that I'd heard and read of Negro children being bitten by rats in their beds. At first I rejected the idea of Bigger battling a rat in his room; I was afraid that the rat would "hog" the scene. But the rat would not leave me; he presented himself in many attractive guises. So, cautioning myself to allow the rat scene to disclose *only* Bigger, his family, their little room, and their relationships, I let the rat walk in, and he did his stuff.

Many of the scenes were torn out as I reworked the book. The mere rereading of what I'd written made me think of the possibility of developing themes which had been only hinted at in the first draft. For example, the entire guilt theme that runs through *Native Son* was woven in *after* the first draft was written.

At last I found out how to end the book; I ended it just as I had begun it, showing Bigger living dangerously, taking his life into his hands, accepting what life had made him. The lawyer, Max, was placed in Bigger's cell at the end of the novel to register the moral—or what *I* felt was the moral—horror of Negro life in the United States.

The writing of *Native Son* was to me an exciting, enthralling, and even a romantic experience. With what I've learned in the writing of this book, with all of its blemishes, imperfections, with all of its unrealized potentialities, I am launching out upon another novel, this time about the status of women in modern American society. This book, too, goes back to my childhood just as Bigger went, for, while I was storing away impressions of Bigger, I was storing away impressions of many other things that made me think and wonder. Some experience will ignite somewhere deep down in me the smoldering embers of new fires and I'll be off again to write yet another novel. It is good to live when one feels that such as that will happen to one. Life becomes sufficient unto life; the rewards of living are found in living.

I don't know if *Native Son* is a good book or a bad book. And I don't know if the book I'm working on now will be a good book or a bad book. And I really don't care. The mere writing of it will be more fun and a deeper satisfaction than any praise or blame from anybody.

I feel that I'm lucky to be alive to write novels today, when the whole world is caught in the pangs of war and change. Early American writers, Henry James and Nathaniel Hawthorne, complained bitterly about the bleakness and flatness of the American scene. But I think that if they were alive, they'd feel at home in modern America. True, we have no great church in America; our national traditions are still of such a sort that we are not wont to brag of them; and we have no army that's above the level of mercenary fighters; we have no group acceptable to the whole of our country upholding certain humane values; we have no rich symbols, no colorful rituals. We have only a money-grubbing industrial civilization. But we do have in the Negro the embodiment of a past tragic enough to appease the spiritual hunger of even a James; and we have in the oppression of the Negro a shadow athwart our national life dense and heavy enough to satisfy even the gloomy broodings of a Hawthorne. And if Poe were alive, he would not have to invent horror; horror would invent him.

Many Thousands Gone

by James Baldwin

It is only in his music, which Americans are able to admire because a protective sentimentality limits their understanding of it, that the Negro in America has been able to tell his story. It is a story which otherwise has yet to be told and which no American is prepared to hear. As is the inevitable result of things unsaid, we find ourselves until today oppressed with a dangerous and reverberating silence; and the story is told, compulsively, in symbols and signs, in hieroglyphics; it is revealed in Negro speech and in that of the white majority and in their different frames of reference. The ways in which the Negro has affected the American psychology are betrayed in our popular culture and in our morality; in our estrangement from him is the depth of our estrangement from ourselves. We cannot ask: what do we *really* feel about him—such a question merely opens the gates on chaos. What we really feel about him is involved with all that we feel about everything, about everyone, about ourselves.

The story of the Negro in America is the story of America—or, more precisely, it is the story of Americans. It is not a very pretty story: the story of a people is never very pretty. The Negro in America, gloomily referred to as that shadow which lies athwart our national life, is far more than that. He is a series of shadows, self-created, intertwining, which now we helplessly battle. One may say that the Negro in America does not really exist except in the darkness of our minds.

This is why his history and his progress, his relationship to all other Americans, has been kept in the social arena. He is a social and not a personal or a human problem; to think of him is to think of statistics, slums, rapes, injustices, remote violence; it is to

be confronted with an endless cataloguing of losses, gains, skir-
mishes; it is to feel virtuous, outraged, helpless, as though his continuing status among us were somehow analogous to disease—can-
cer, perhaps, or tuberculosis—which must be checked, even though
it cannot be cured. In this arena the black man acquires quite
another aspect from that which he has in life. We do not know
what to do with him in life; if he breaks our sociological and sentimental image of him we are panic-stricken and we feel ourselves
betrayed. When he violates this image, therefore, he stands in the
greatest danger (sensing which, we uneasily suspect that he is very
often playing a part for our benefit); and, what is not always so
apparent but is equally true, we are then in some danger ourselves
—hence our retreat or our blind and immediate retaliation.

Our dehumanization of the Negro then is indivisible from our
dehumanization of ourselves: the loss of our own identity is the
price we pay for our annulment of his. Time and our own force
act as our allies, creating an impossible, a fruitless tension between
the traditional master and slave. Impossible and fruitless because,
literal and visible as this tension has become, it has nothing to do
with reality.

Time has made some changes in the Negro face. Nothing has
succeeded in making it exactly like our own, though the general
desire seems to be to make it blank if one cannot make it white.
When it has become blank, the past as thoroughly washed from
the black face as it has been from ours, our guilt will be finished—
at least it will have ceased to be visible, which we imagine to be
much the same thing. But, paradoxically, it is we who prevent this
from happening; since it is we, who, every hour that we live, re-
invest the black face with our guilt; and we do this—by a further
paradox, no less ferocious—helplessly, passionately, out of an unrealized need to suffer absolution.

Today, to be sure, we know that the Negro is not biologically or
mentally inferior; there is no truth in those rumors of his body
odor or his incorrigible sexuality; or no more truth than can be
easily explained or even defended by the social sciences. Yet, in our
most recent war, his blood was segregated as was, for the most part,
his person. Up to today we are set at a division, so that he may not
marry our daughters or our sisters, nor may he—for the most part
—eat at our tables or live in our houses. Moreover, those who do,
do so at the grave expense of a double alienation: from their own
people, whose fabled attributes they must either deny or, worse,

cheapen and bring to market; from us, for we require of them, when we accept them, that they at once cease to be Negroes and yet not fail to remember what being a Negro means—to remember, that is, what it means to us. The threshold of insult is higher or lower, according to the people involved, from the bootblack in Atlanta to the celebrity in New York. One must travel very far, among saints with nothing to gain or outcasts with nothing to lose, to find a place where it does not matter—and perhaps a word or a gesture or simply a silence will testify that it matters even there.

For it means something to be a Negro, after all, as it means something to have been born in Ireland or in China, to live where one sees space and sky or to live where one sees nothing but rubble or nothing but high buildings. We cannot escape our origins, however hard we try, those origins which contain the key—could we but find it—to all that we later become. What it means to be a Negro is a good deal more than this essay can discover; what it means to be a Negro in America can perhaps be suggested by an examination of the myths we perpetuate about him.

Aunt Jemima and Uncle Tom are dead, their places taken by a group of amazingly well-adjusted young men and women, almost as dark, but ferociously literate, well-dressed and scrubbed, who are never laughed at, who are not likely ever to set foot in a cotton or tobacco field or in any but the most modern of kitchens. There are others who remain, in our odd idiom, "underprivileged"; some are bitter and these come to grief; some are unhappy, but, continually presented with the evidence of a better day soon to come, are speedily becoming less so. Most of them care nothing whatever about race. They want only their proper place in the sun and the right to be left alone, like any other citizen of the republic. We may all breathe more easily. Before, however, our joy at the demise of Aunt Jemima and Uncle Tom approaches the indecent, we had better ask whence they sprang, how they lived? Into what limbo have they vanished?

However inaccurate our portraits of them were, these portraits do suggest, not only the conditions, but the quality of their lives and the impact of this spectacle on our consciences. There was no one more forbearing than Aunt Jemima, no one stronger or more pious or more loyal or more wise; there was, at the same time, no one weaker or more faithless or more vicious and certainly no one more immoral. Uncle Tom, trustworthy and sexless, needed only to drop the title "Uncle" to become violent, crafty, and sullen, a menace to any white woman who passed by. They prepared our feast tables and our burial clothes; and, if we could boast that we understood them, it was far more to the point and far more true that they understood us. They were, moreover, the only people in the world who did; and not only did they know us better than we knew ourselves, but they knew us better than we knew them. This was the piquant flavoring to the national joke, it lay behind our uneasiness as it lay behind our benevolence: Aunt Jemima and Uncle Tom, our creations, at the last evaded us; they had a life— their own, perhaps a better life than ours—and they would never tell us what it was. At the point where we were driven most privately and painfully to conjecture what depths of contempt, what heights of indifference, what prodigies of resilience, what untamable superiority allowed them so vividly to endure, neither perishing nor rising up in a body to wipe us from the earth, the image perpetually shattered and the word failed. The black man in our midst carried murder in his heart, he wanted vengeance. We carried murder too, we wanted peace.

In our image of the Negro breathes the past we deny, not dead but living yet and powerful, the beast in our jungle of statistics. It is this which defeats us, which continues to defeat us, which lends to interracial cocktail parties their rattling, genteel, nervously smiling air: in any drawing room at such a gathering the beast may spring, filling the air with flying things and an unenlightened wailing. Wherever the problem touches there is confusion, there is danger. Wherever the Negro face appears a tension is created, the tension of a silence filled with things unutterable. It is a sentimental error, therefore, to believe that the past is dead; it means nothing to say that it is all forgotten, that the Negro himself has forgotten it. It is not a question of memory. Oedipus did not remember the thongs that bound his feet; nevertheless the marks they left testified to that doom toward which his feet were leading him. The man does not remember the hand that struck him, the darkness that frightened him, as a child; nevertheless, the hand and the darkness remain with him, indivisible from himself forever, part of the passion that drives him wherever he thinks to take flight.

The making of an American begins at that point where he himself rejects all other ties, any other history, and himself adopts the vesture of his adopted land. This problem has been faced by all Americans throughout our history—in a way it *is* our history—and

it baffles the immigrant and sets on edge the second generation
until today. In the case of the Negro the past was taken from him
whether he would or no; yet to forswear it was meaningless and
availed him nothing, since his shameful history was carried, quite
literally, on his brow. Shameful; for he was heathen as well as
black and would never have discovered the healing blood of Christ
had not we braved the jungles to bring him these glad tidings.
Shameful; for, since our role as missionary had not been wholly
disinterested, it was necessary to recall the shame from which we
had delivered him in order more easily to escape our own. As he
accepted the alabaster Christ and the bloody cross—in the bearing
of which he would find his redemption, as, indeed, to our outraged
astonishment, he sometimes did—he must, henceforth, accept that
image we then gave him of himself: having no other and standing,
moreover, in danger of death should he fail to accept the dazzling
light thus brought into such darkness. It is this quite simple dilemma that must be borne in mind if we wish to comprehend his
psychology.

However we shift the light which beats so fiercely on his head,
or *prove*, by victorious social analysis, how his lot has changed, how
we have both improved, our uneasiness refuses to be exorcized. And
nowhere is this more apparent than in our literature on the subject—"problem" literature when written by whites, "protest" literature when written by Negroes—and nothing is more striking
than the tremendous disparity of tone between the two creations.
Kingsblood Royal bears, for example, almost no kinship to *If He
Hollers Let Him Go*, though the same reviewers praised them both
for what were, at bottom, very much the same reasons. These reasons may be suggested, far too briefly but not at all unjustly, by
observing that the presupposition is in both novels exactly the
same: black is a terrible color with which to be born into the world.

Now the most powerful and celebrated statement we have yet
had of what it means to be a Negro in America is unquestionably
Richard Wright's *Native Son*. The feeling which prevailed at the
time of its publication was that such a novel, bitter, uncompromis-
ing, shocking, gave proof, by its very existence, of what strides
might be taken in a free democracy; and its indisputable success,
proof that Americans were now able to look full in the face without flinching the dreadful facts. Americans, unhappily, have the
most remarkable ability to alchemize all bitter truths into an in-
nocuous but piquant confection and to transform their moral con-

tradictions, or public discussion of such contradictions, into a proud decoration, such as are given for heroism on the field of battle. Such a book, we felt with pride, could never have been written before— which was true. Nor could it be written today. It bears already the aspect of a landmark; for Bigger and his brothers have undergone yet another metamorphosis; they have been accepted in baseball leagues and by colleges hitherto exclusive; and they have made a most favorable appearance on the national screen. We have yet to encounter, nevertheless, a report so indisputably authentic, or one that can begin to challenge this most significant novel.

It is, in a certain American tradition, the story of an unremarkable youth in battle with the force of circumstance; that force of circumstance which plays and which has played so important a part in the national fables of success or failure. In this case the force of circumstance is not poverty merely but color, a circumstance which cannot be overcome, against which the protagonist battles for his life and loses. It is, on the surface, remarkable that this book should have enjoyed among Americans the favor it did enjoy; no more remarkable, however, than that it should have been compared, exuberantly, to Dostoevsky, though placed a shade below Dos Passos, Dreiser, and Steinbeck; and when the book is examined, its impact does not seem remarkable at all, but becomes, on the contrary, perfectly logical and inevitable.

We cannot, to begin with, divorce this book from the specific social climate of that time: it was one of the last of those angry productions, encountered in the late twenties and all through the thirties, dealing with the inequities of the social structure of America. It was published one year before our entry into the last world war—which is to say, very few years after the dissolution of the WPA and the end of the New Deal and at a time when bread lines and soup kitchens and bloody industrial battles were bright in everyone's memory. The rigors of that unexpected time filled us not only with a genuinely bewildered and despairing idealism—so that, because there at least was *something* to fight for, young men went off to die in Spain—but also with a genuinely bewildered self-consciousness. The Negro, who had been during the magnificent twenties a passionate and delightful primitive, now became, as one of the things we were most self-conscious about, our most oppressed minority. In the thirties, swallowing Marx whole, we discovered the Worker and realized—I should think with some relief—that the aims of the Worker and the aims of the Negro were one. This the-

orem—to which we shall return—seems now to leave rather too
much out of account; it became, nevertheless, one of the slogans of
the "class struggle" and the gospel of the New Negro.

As for this New Negro, it was Wright who became his most eloquent spokesman; and his work, from its beginning, is most clearly
committed to the social struggle. Leaving aside the considerable
question of what relationship precisely the artist bears to the revolutionary, the reality of man as a social being is not his only reality
and that artist is strangled who is forced to deal with human beings
solely in social terms; and who has, moreover, as Wright had, the
necessity thrust on him of being the representative of some thirteen
million people. It is a false responsibility (since writers are not
congressmen) and impossible, by its nature, of fulfillment. The un-
lucky shepherd soon finds that, so far from being able to feed the
hungry sheep, he has lost the wherewithal for his own nourishment:
having not been allowed—so fearful was his burden, so present his
audience!—to recreate his own experience. Further, the militant
men and women of the thirties were not, upon examination, significantly emancipated from their antecedents, however bitterly they
might consider themselves estranged or however gallantly they
struggled to build a better world. However they might extol Russia, their concept of a better world was quite helplessly American
and betrayed a certain thinness of imagination, a suspect reliance
on suspect and badly digested formulae, and a positively fretful
romantic haste. Finally, the relationship of the Negro to the Worker
cannot be summed up, nor even greatly illuminated, by saying that
their aims are one. It is true only insofar as they both desire better
working conditions and useful only insofar as they unite their
strength as workers to achieve these ends. Further than this we cannot in honesty go.

In this climate Wright's voice first was heard and the struggle
which promised for a time to shape his work and give it purpose
also fixed it in an ever more unrewarding rage. Recording his days
of anger he has also nevertheless recorded, as no Negro before him
had ever done, that fantasy Americans hold in their minds when
they speak of the Negro: that fantastic and fearful image which
we have lived with since the first slave fell beneath the lash. This
is the significance of *Native Son* and also, unhappily, its overwhelming limitation.

Native Son begins with the *Brring!* of an alarm clock in the squalid Chicago tenement where Bigger and his family live. Rats live there too, feeding off the garbage, and we first encounter Bigger in the act of killing one. One may consider that the entire book, from that harsh *Brring!* to Bigger's weak "Good-by" as the lawyer, Max, leaves him in the death cell, is an extension, with the roles inverted, of this chilling metaphor. Bigger's situation and Bigger himself exert on the mind the same sort of fascination. The premise of the book is, as I take it, clearly conveyed in these first pages: we are confronting a monster created by the American republic and we are, through being made to share his experience, to receive illumination as regards the manner of his life and to feel both pity and horror at his awful and inevitable doom. This is an arresting and potentially rich idea and we would be discussing a very different novel if Wright's execution had been more perceptive and if he had not attempted to redeem a symbolical monster in social terms.

One may object that it was precisely Wright's intention to create in Bigger a social symbol, revelatory of social disease and prophetic of disaster. I think, however, that it is this assumption which we ought to examine more carefully. Bigger has no discernible relationship to himself, to his own life, to his own people, nor to any other people—in this respect, perhaps, he is most American—and his force comes, not from his significance as a social (or anti-social) unit, but from his significance as the incarnation of a myth. It is remarkable that, though we follow him step by step from the tenement room to the death cell, we know as little about him when this journey is ended as we did when it began; and, what is even more remarkable, we know almost as little about the social dynamic which we are to believe created him. Despite the details of slum life which we are given, I doubt that anyone who has thought about it, disengaging himself from sentimentality, can accept this most essential premise of the novel for a moment. Those Negroes who surround him, on the other hand, his hard-working mother, his ambitious sister, his poolroom cronies, Bessie, might be considered as far richer and far more subtle and accurate illustrations of the ways in which Negroes are controlled in our society and the complex techniques they have evolved for their survival. We are limited, however, to Bigger's view of them, part of a deliberate plan which might not have been disastrous if we were not also limited to Bigger's perceptions. What this means for the novel is that a necessary dimension has been cut away; this dimension being the relationship that Negroes bear to one another, that depth of involvement and unspoken recognition of shared experience which creates a way of life. What the novel reflects—and at no point interprets—is the isolation of the Negro within his own group and the resulting fury of impatient scorn. It is this which creates its climate of anarchy and unmotivated and unapprehended disaster; and it is this climate, common to most Negro protest novels, which has led us all to believe that in Negro life there exists no tradition, no field of manners, no possibility of ritual or intercourse, such as may, for example, sustain the Jew even after he has left his father's house. But the fact is not that the Negro has no tradition but that there has as yet arrived no sensibility sufficiently profound and tough to make this tradition articulate. For a tradition expresses, after all, nothing more than the long and painful experience of a people; it comes out of the battle waged to maintain their integrity or, to put it more simply, out of their struggle to survive. When we speak of the Jewish tradition we are speaking of centuries of exile and persecution, of the strength which endured and the sensibility which discovered in it the high possibility of the moral victory.

This sense of how Negroes live and how they have so long endured is hidden from us in part by the very speed of the Negro's public progress, a progress so heavy with complexity, so bewildering and kaleidoscopic, that he dare not pause to conjecture on the darkness which lies behind him; and by the nature of the American psychology which, in order to apprehend or be made able to accept it, must undergo a metamorphosis so profound as to be literally unthinkable and which there is no doubt we will resist until we are compelled to achieve our own identity by the rigors of a time that has yet to come. Bigger, in the meanwhile, and all his furious kin, serve only to whet the notorious national taste for the sensational and to reinforce all that we now find it necessary to believe. It is not Bigger whom we fear, since his appearance among us makes our victory certain. It is the others, who smile, who go to church, who give no cause for complaint, whom we sometimes consider with amusement, with pity, even with affection—and in whose faces we sometimes surprise the merest arrogant hint of hatred, the faintest, withdrawn, speculative shadow of contempt—who make us uneasy; whom we cajole, threaten, flatter, fear; who to us remain unknown, though we are not (we feel with both relief and hostility and with bottomless confusion) unknown to them. It is out of our reaction to these hewers of wood and drawers of water that our image of Bigger was created.

It is this image, living yet, which we perpetually seek to evade with good works; and this image which makes of all our good works an intolerable mockery. The "nigger," black, benighted, brutal, consumed with hatred as we are consumed with guilt, cannot be thus blotted out. He stands at our shoulders when we give our maid her wages, it is his hand which we fear we are taking when struggling to communicate with the current "intelligent" Negro, his stench, as it were, which fills our mouths with salt as the monument is unveiled in honor of the latest Negro leader. Each generation has shouted behind him, *Nigger!* as he walked our streets; it is he whom we would rather our sisters did not marry; he is banished into the vast and wailing outer darkness whenever we speak of the "purity" of our women, of the "sanctity" of our homes, of "American" ideals. What is more, he knows it. He is indeed the "native son": he is the "nigger." Let us refrain from inquiring at the moment whether or not he actually exists; for we *believe* that he exists. Whenever we encounter him amongst us in the flesh, our faith is made perfect and his necessary and bloody end is executed with a mystical ferocity of joy.

But there is a complementary faith among the damned which involves their gathering of the stones with which those who walk in the light shall stone them; or there exists among the intolerably degraded the perverse and powerful desire to force into the arena of the actual those fantastic crimes of which they have been accused, achieving their vengeance and their own destruction through making the nightmare real. The American image of the Negro lives also in the Negro's heart; and when he has surrendered to this image life has no other possible reality. Then he, like the white enemy with whom he will be locked one day in mortal struggle, has no means save this of asserting his identity. This is why Bigger's murder of Mary can be referred to as an "act of creation" and why, once this murder has been committed, he can feel for the first time that he is living fully and deeply as a man was meant to live. And there is, I should think, no Negro living in America who has not felt, briefly or for long periods, with anguish sharp or dull, in varying degrees and to varying effect, simple, naked and unanswerable hatred; who has not wanted to smash any white face he may encounter in a day, to violate, out of motives of the cruelest vengeance, their women, to break the bodies of all white people and bring them low, as low as that dust into which he himself has been and is being trampled; no Negro, finally, who has not had to make his own precarious adjustment to the "nigger" who surrounds him and to the "nigger" in himself.

Yet the adjustment must be made—rather, it must be attempted, the tension perpetually sustained—for without this he has surrendered his birthright as a man no less than his birthright as a black man. The entire universe is then peopled only with his enemies, who are not only white men armed with rope and rifle, but his own far-flung and contemptible kinsmen. Their blackness is his degradation and it is their stupid and passive endurance which makes his end inevitable.

Bigger dreams of some black man who will weld all blacks together into a mighty fist, and feels, in relation to his family, that perhaps they had to live as they did precisely because none of them had ever done anything, right or wrong, which mattered very much. It is only he who, by an act of murder, has burst the dungeon cell. He has made it manifest that *he* lives and that his despised blood nourishes the passions of a man. He has forced his oppressors to see the fruit of that oppression: and he feels, when his family and his friends come to visit him in the death cell, that they should not be weeping or frightened, that they should be happy, *proud* that he has dared, through murder and now through his own imminent destruction, to redeem their anger and humiliation, that he has hurled into the spiritless obscurity of their lives the lamp of his passionate life and death. Henceforth, they may remember Bigger—who has died, as we may conclude, for them. But they do not feel this; they only know that he has murdered two women and precipitated a reign of terror; and that now he is to die in the electric chair. They therefore weep and are honestly frightened—for which Bigger despises them and wishes to "blot" them out. What is missing in his situation and in the representation of his psychology—which makes his situation false and his psychology incapable of development—is any revelatory apprehension of Bigger as one of the Negro's realities or as one of the Negro's roles. This failure is part of the previously noted failure to convey any sense of Negro life as a continuing and complex group reality. Bigger, who cannot function therefore as a reflection of the social illness, having, as it were, no society to reflect, likewise refuses to function on the loftier level of the Christ-symbol. His kinsmen are quite right to weep and be frightened, even to be appalled: for it is not his love for them or for himself which causes him to die, but his hatred and his self-hatred; he does not redeem the pains of a despised people, but reveals, on the contrary, nothing more than his own fierce bitterness at having been born one of them. In this also he is the "native son," his progress determinable by the speed with which the distance increases between himself and the auction-block and all that the auction-block implies. To have penetrated this phenomenon, this inward contention of love and hatred, blackness and whiteness, would have given him a stature more nearly human and an end more nearly tragic; and would have given us a document more profoundly and genuinely bitter and less harsh with an anger which is, on the one hand, exhibited and, on the other hand, denied.

Native Son finds itself at length so trapped by the American image of Negro life and by the American necessity to find the ray of hope that it cannot pursue its own implications. This is why Bigger must be at the last redeemed, to be received, if only by rhetoric, into that community of phantoms which is our tenaciously held ideal of the happy social life. It is the socially conscious whites who receive him—the Negroes being capable of no such objectivity—and we have, by way of illustration, that lamentable scene in which Jan, Mary's lover, forgives him for her murder; and, carrying the explicit burden of the novel, Max's long speech to the jury. This speech, which really ends the book, is one of the most desperate performances in American fiction. It is the question of Bigger's humanity which is at stake, the relationship in which he stands to all other Americans—and, by implication, to all people—and it is precisely this question which it cannot clarify, with which it cannot, in fact, come to any coherent terms. He is the monster created by the American republic, the present awful sum of generations of oppression; but to say that he is a monster is to fall into the trap of making him subhuman and he must, therefore, be made representative of a way of life which is real and human in precise ratio to the degree to which it seems to us monstrous and strange. It seems to me that this idea carries, implicitly, a most remarkable confession: that is, that Negro life is in fact as debased and impoverished as our theology claims; and, further, that the use to which Wright puts this idea can only proceed from the assumption—not entirely unsound—that Americans, who evade, so far as possible, all genuine experience, have therefore no way of assessing the experience of others and no way of establishing themselves in relation to any way of life which is not their own. The privacy or obscurity of Negro life makes that life capable, in our imaginations, of producing anything at all; and thus the idea of Bigger's monstrosity can be presented without fear of contradiction, since no American has the knowledge or authority to contest it and no Negro has the voice. It is an idea, which, in the framework of the novel, is dignified by the possibility it promptly affords of presenting Bigger as the herald of disaster, the danger signal of a more bitter time to come when not Bigger alone but all his kindred will rise, in the name of the many thousands who have perished in fire and flood and by rope and torture, to demand their rightful vengeance.

But it is not quite fair, it seems to me, to exploit the national innocence in this way. The idea of Bigger as a warning boomerangs not only because it is quite beyond the limit of probability that Negroes in America will ever achieve the means of wreaking vengeance upon the state but also because it cannot be said that they have any desire to do so. *Native Son* does not convey the altogether savage paradox of the American Negro's situation, of which the social reality which we prefer with such hopeful superficiality to study is but, as it were, the shadow. It is not simply the relationship of oppressed to oppressor, of master to slave, nor is it motivated merely by hatred; it is also, literally and morally, a *blood* relationship, perhaps the most profound reality of the American experience, and we cannot begin to unlock it until we accept how very much it contains of the force and anguish and terror of love.

Negroes are Americans and their destiny is the country's destiny. They have no other experience besides their experience on this continent and it is an experience which cannot be rejected, which yet remains to be embraced. If, as I believe, no American Negro exists who does not have his private Bigger Thomas living in the skull, then what most significantly fails to be illuminated here is the paradoxical adjustment which is perpetually made, the Negro being compelled to accept the fact that this dark and dangerous and unloved stranger is part of himself forever. Only this recognition sets him in any wise free and it is this, this necessary ability to contain and even, in the most honorable sense of the word, to *exploit* the "nigger," which lends to Negro life its high element of the ironic and which causes the most well-meaning of their American critics to make such exhilarating errors when attempting to understand them. To present Bigger as a warning is simply to reinforce the American guilt and fear concerning him, it is most forcefully to limit him to that previously mentioned social arena in which he has no human validity, it is simply to condemn him to death. For he has always been a warning, he represents evil, the sin and suffering which we are compelled to reject. It is useless to say to the courtroom in which this heathen sits on trial that he is their responsibility, their creation, and his crimes are theirs; and that they ought, therefore, to allow him to live, to make articulate to himself behind the walls of prison the meaning of his existence. The meaning of his existence has already been most adequately expressed, nor does anyone wish, particularly not in the name of democracy, to think of it any more; as for the possibility of articulation, it is this possibility which above all others we most dread. Moreover, the courtroom, judge, jury, witnesses and spectators, recognize immediately that Bigger is their creation and they recognize this not only with hatred and fear and guilt and the resulting fury of self-righteousness but also with that morbid fullness of pride mixed with horror with which one regards the extent and power of one's wickedness. They know that death is his portion, that he runs to death; coming from darkness and dwelling in darkness, he must be, as often as he rises, banished, lest the entire planet be engulfed. And they know, finally, that they do not wish to forgive him and that he does not wish to be forgiven; that he dies, hating them, scorning that appeal which they cannot make to that irrecoverable humanity of his which cannot hear it; and that he *wants* to die because he glories in his hatred and prefers, like Lucifer, rather to rule in hell than serve in heaven.

For, bearing in mind the premise on which the life of such a man is based, i.e., that black is the color of damnation, this is his only possible end. It is the only death which will allow him a kind of dignity or even, however horribly, a kind of beauty. To tell this story, no more than a single aspect of the story of the "nigger," is inevitably and richly to become involved with the force of life and legend, how each perpetually assumes the guise of the other, creating that dense, many-sided and shifting reality which is the world we live in and the world we make. To tell his story is to begin to liberate us from his image and it is, for the first time, to clothe this phantom with flesh and blood, to deepen, by our understanding of him and his relationship to us, our understanding of ourselves and of all men.

But this is not the story which *Native Son* tells, for we find here merely, repeated in anger, the story which we have told in pride. Nor, since the implications of this anger are evaded, are we ever confronted with the actual or potential significance of our pride; which is why we fall, with such a positive glow of recognition, upon Max's long and bitter summing up. It is addressed to those among us of good will and it seems to say that, though there are whites and blacks among us who hate each other, we will not; there are those who are betrayed by greed, by guilt, by blood lust, but not we; we will set our faces against them and join hands and walk together into that dazzling future when there will be no white or black. This is the dream of all liberal men, a dream not at all dishonorable, but, nevertheless, a dream. For, let us join hands on this mountain as we may, the battle is elsewhere. It proceeds far from us in the heat and horror and pain of life itself where all men are betrayed by greed and guilt and blood lust and where no one's hands are clean. Our good will, from which we yet expect such power to transform us, is thin, passionless, strident: its roots, examined, lead us back to our forebears, whose assumption it was that the black man, to become truly human and acceptable, must first become like us. This assumption once accepted, the Negro in America can only acquiesce in the obliteration of his own personality, the distortion and debasement of his own experience, surrendering to those forces which reduce the person to anonymity and which make themselves manifest daily all over the darkening world.

Black Boys and Native Sons

by Irving Howe

. . . The day *Native Son* appeared, American culture was changed forever. No matter how much qualifying the book might later need, it made impossible a repetition of the old lies. In all its crudeness, melodrama and claustrophobia of vision, Richard Wright's novel brought out into the open, as no one ever had before, the hatred, fear and violence that have crippled and may yet destroy our culture.

A blow at the white man, the novel forced him to recognize himself as an oppressor. A blow at the black man, the novel forced him to recognize the cost of his submission. *Native Son* assaulted the most cherished of American vanities: the hope that the accumulated injustice of the past would bring with it no lasting penalties, the fantasy that in his humiliation the Negro somehow retained a sexual potency—or was it a childlike good-nature?—that made it necessary to envy and still more to suppress him. Speaking from the black wrath of retribution, Wright insisted that history can be a punishment. He told us the one thing even the most liberal whites preferred not to hear: that Negroes were far from patient or forgiving, that they were scarred by fear, that they hated every moment of their suppression even when seeming most acquiescent, and that often enough they hated *us*, the decent and cultivated white men who from complicity or neglect shared in the responsibility for their plight. If such younger novelists as Baldwin and Ralph Ellison were to move beyond Wright's harsh naturalism and toward

From "Black Boys and Native Sons" in A World More Attractive, *by Irving Howe (New York: Horizon Press, 1963), pp. 100–110. Copyright © 1963 by Irving Howe. Reprinted by permission of the publisher, Horizon Press, New York.*

The original essay deals with Wright, Baldwin, and Ellison and their relationship to a viable literary tradition. Omissions are indicated by ellipses. Howe's essay should be read in conjunction with Ralph Ellison's reply, which appears as "The World and the Jug," Shadow and Act *(New York: Signet, 1966), pp. 115–47.*

more supple modes of fiction, that was possible only because Wright
had been there first, courageous enough to release the full weight
of his anger.

In *Black Boy,* the autobiographical narrative he published several
years later, Wright would tell of an experience he had while working as a bellboy in the South. Many times he had come into a hotel
room carrying luggage or food and seen naked white women loung-
ing about, unmoved by shame at his presence, for "blacks were not
considered human beings anyway . . . I was a non-man . . . I felt
doubly cast out." With the publication of *Native Son,* however,
Wright forced his readers to acknowledge his anger, and in that
way, if none other, he wrested for himself a sense of dignity as a
man. He forced his readers to confront the disease of our culture,
and to one of its most terrifying symptoms he gave the name of
Bigger Thomas.

Brutal and brutalized, lost forever to his unexpended hatred and
his fear of the world, a numbed and illiterate black boy stumbling
into a murder and never, not even at the edge of the electric chair,
breaking through to an understanding of either his plight or himself, Bigger Thomas was a part of Richard Wright, a part even of
the James Baldwin who stared with horror at Wright's Bigger, unable either to absorb him into his consciousness or eject him from
it. Enormous courage, a discipline of self-conquest, was required to
conceive Bigger Thomas, for this was no eloquent Negro spokesman, no admirable intellectual or formidable proletarian. Bigger
was drawn—one would surmise, deliberately—from white fantasy
and white contempt. Bigger was the worst of Negro life accepted,
then rendered a trifle conscious and thrown back at those who had
made him what he was. "No American Negro exists," Baldwin
would later write, "who does not have his private Bigger Thomas
living in the skull."

Wright drove his narrative to the very core of American phobia:
sexual fright, sexual violation. He understood that the fantasy of
rape is a consequence of guilt, what the whites suppose themselves
to deserve. He understood that the white man's notion of uncon-
taminated Negro vitality, little as it had to do with the bitter realities of Negro life, reflected some ill-formed and buried feeling that
our culture has run down, losts its blood, become febrile. And he
grasped the way in which the sexual issue has been intertwined
with social relationships, for even as the white people who hire
Bigger as their chauffeur are decent and charitable, even as the girl

he accidentally kills is a liberal of sorts, theirs is the power and the privilege. "We black and they white. They got things and we ain't. They do things and we can't."

The novel barely stops to provision a recognizable social world, often contenting itself with cartoon simplicities and yielding almost entirely to the nightmare incomprehension of Bigger Thomas. The mood is apocalyptic, the tone superbly aggressive. Wright was an existentialist long before he heard the name, for he was committed to the literature of extreme situations both through the pressures of his rage and the gasping hope of an ultimate catharsis.

Wright confronts both the violence and the crippling limitations of Bigger Thomas. For Bigger white people are not people at all, but something more, "a sort of great natural force, like a stormy sky looming overhead." And only through violence does he gather a little meaning in life, pitifully little: "he had murdered and created a new life for himself." Beyond that Bigger cannot go.

At first *Native Son* seems still another naturalistic novel: a novel of exposure and accumulation, charting the waste of the undersides of the American city. Behind the book one senses the molding influence of Theodore Dreiser, especially the Dreiser of *An American Tragedy* who knows there are situations so oppressive that only violence can provide their victims with the hope of dignity. Like Dreiser, Wright wished to pummel his readers into awareness; like Dreiser, to overpower them with the sense of society as an enclosing force. Yet the comparison is finally of limited value, and for the disconcerting reason that Dreiser had a white skin and Wright a black one.

The usual naturalistic novel is written with detachment, as if by a scientist surveying a field of operations; it is a novel in which the writer withdraws from a detested world and coldly piles up the evidence for detesting it. *Native Son*, though preserving some of the devices of the naturalistic novel, deviates sharply from its characteristic tone: a tone Wright could not possibly have maintained and which, it may be, no Negro novelist can really hold for long. *Native Son* is a work of assault rather than withdrawal; the author yields himself in part to a vision of nightmare. Bigger's cowering perception of the world becomes the most vivid and authentic component of the book. Naturalism pushed to an extreme turns here into something other than itself, a kind of expressionist outburst, no longer a replica of the familiar social world but a self-contained realm of grotesque emblems.

That *Native Son* has grave faults anyone can see. The language is often coarse, flat in rhythm, syntactically overburdened, heavy with journalistic slag. Apart from Bigger, who seems more a brute energy than a particularized figure, the characters have little reality, the Negroes being mere stock accessories and the whites either "agit-prop" villains or heroic Communists whom Wright finds it easier to admire from a distance than establish from the inside. The long speech by Bigger's radical lawyer Max (again a device apparently borrowed from Dreiser) is ill-related to the book itself: Wright had not achieved Dreiser's capacity for absorbing everything, even the most recalcitrant philosophical passages, into a unified vision of things. Between Wright's feelings as a Negro and his beliefs as a Communist there is hardly a genuine fusion, and it is through this gap that a good part of the novel's unreality pours in.

Yet it should be said that the endlessly repeated criticism that Wright caps his melodrama with a party-line oration tends to over-simplify the novel, for Wright is too honest simply to allow the propagandistic message to constitute the last word. Indeed, the last word is given not to Max but to Bigger. For at the end Bigger remains at the mercy of his hatred and fear, the lawyer retreats help-lessly, the projected union between political consciousness and raw revolt has not been achieved—as if Wright were persuaded that, all ideology apart, there is for each Negro an ultimate trial that he can bear only by himself.

Black Boy, which appeared five years after *Native Son,* is a slighter but more skillful piece of writing. Richard Wright came from a broken home, and as he moved from his helpless mother to a grandmother whose religious fanaticism (she was a Seventh-Day Adventist) proved utterly suffocating, he soon picked up a preco-cious knowledge of vice and a realistic awareness of social power. This autobiographical memoir, a small classic in the literature of self-discovery, is packed with harsh evocations of Negro adolescence in the South. The young Wright learns how wounding it is to wear the mask of a grinning niggerboy in order to keep a job. He exam-ines the life of the Negroes and judges it without charity or idyllic compensation—for he already knows, in his heart and his bones, that to be oppressed means to lose out on human possibilities. By the time he is seventeen, preparing to leave for Chicago, where he will work on a WPA project, become a member of the Commu-nist Party, and publish his first book of stories called *Uncle Tom's Children,* Wright has managed to achieve the beginnings of consciousness, through a slow and painful growth from the very bottom of deprivation to the threshold of artistic achievement and a glimpsed idea of freedom.

Baldwin's attack upon Wright had partly been anticipated by the more sophisticated American critics. Alfred Kazin, for example, had found in Wright a troubling obsession with violence:

> If he chose to write the story of Bigger Thomas as a grotesque crime story, it is because his own indignation and the sickness of the age combined to make him dependent on violence and shock, to astonish the reader by torrential scenes of cruelty, hunger, rape, murder and flight, and then enlighten him by crude Stalinist homilies.

The last phrase apart, something quite similar could be said about the author of *Crime and Punishment;* it is disconcerting to reflect upon how few novelists, even the very greatest, could pass this kind of moral inspection. For the novel as a genre seems to have an inherent bias toward extreme effects, such as violence, cruelty and the like. More important, Kazin's judgment rests on the assumption that a critic can readily distinguish between the genuine need of a writer to cope with ugly realities and the damaging effect these realities may have upon his moral and psychic life. But in regard to contemporary writers one finds it very had to distinguish between a valid portrayal of violence and an obsessive involvement with it. A certain amount of obsession may be necessary for the valid portrayal—writers devoted to themes of desperation cannot keep themselves morally intact. And when we come to a writer like Richard Wright, who deals with the most degraded and inarticulate sector of the Negro world, the distinction between objective rendering and subjective immersion becomes still more difficult, perhaps even impossible. For a novelist who has lived through the searing experiences that Wright has there cannot be much possibility of approaching his subject with the "mature" poise recommended by high-minded critics. What is more, the very act of writing his novel, the effort to confront what Bigger Thomas means to him, is for such a writer a way of dredging up and then perhaps shedding the violence that society has pounded into him. Is Bigger an authentic projection of a social reality, or is he a symptom of Wright's "dependence on violence and shock?" Obviously both; and it could not be otherwise.

For the reality pressing upon all of Wright's work was a nightmare of remembrance, everything from which he had pulled himself out, with an effort and at a cost that is almost unimaginable. Without the terror of that nightmare it would have been impossible for Wright to summon the truth of the reality—not the only truth about American Negroes, perhaps not even the deepest one, but a primary and inescapable truth. Both truth and terror rested on a gross fact which Wright alone dared to confront: that violence is a central fact in the life of the American Negro, defining and crippling him with a harshness few other Americans need suffer. "No American Negro exists who does not have his private Bigger Thomas living in the skull."

Now I think it would be well not to judge in the abstract, or with much haste, the violence that gathers in the Negro's heart as a response to the violence he encounters in society. It would be well to see this violence as part of an historical experience that is open to moral scrutiny but ought to be shielded from presumptuous moralizing. Bigger Thomas may be enslaved to a hunger for violence, but anyone reading *Native Son* with mere courtesy must observe the way in which Wright, even while yielding emotionally to Bigger's deprivation, also struggles to transcend it. That he did not fully succeed seems obvious; one may doubt that any Negro writer can.

More subtle and humane than either Kazin's or Baldwin's criticism is a remark made by Isaac Rosenfeld while reviewing *Black Boy*: "As with all Negroes and all men who are born to suffer social injustice, part of [Wright's] humanity found itself only in acquaintance with violence, and in hatred of the oppressor." Surely Rosenfeld was not here inviting an easy acquiescence in violence; he was trying to suggest the historical context, the psychological dynamics, which condition the attitudes all Negro writers take, or must take, toward violence. To say this is not to propose the condescension of exempting Negro writers from moral judgment, but to suggest the terms of understanding, and still more, the terms of hesitation for making a judgment.

There were times when Baldwin grasped this point better than anyone else. If he could speak of the "unrewarding rage" of *Native Son,* he also spoke of the book as "an immense liberation." Is it impudent to suggest that one reason he felt the book to be a liberation was precisely its rage, precisely the relief and pleasure that he, like so many other Negroes, must have felt upon seeing those long-suppressed emotions finally breaking through?

The kind of literary criticism Baldwin wrote was very fashionable in America during the post-war years. Mimicking the Freudian corrosion of motives and bristling with dialectical agility, this criticism approached all ideal claims, especially those made by radical and naturalist writers, with a weary skepticism and proceeded to transfer the values such writers were attacking to the perspective from which they attacked. If Dreiser wrote about the power hunger and dream of success corrupting American society, that was because he was really infatuated with them. If Farrell showed the meanness of life in the Chicago slums, that was because he could not really escape it. If Wright portrayed the violence gripping Negro life, that was because he was really obsessed with it. The word "really" or more sophisticated equivalents could do endless service in behalf of a generation of intellectuals soured on the tradition of protest but suspecting they might be pigmies in comparison to the writers who had protested. In reply, there was no way to "prove" that Dreiser, Farrell and Wright were not contaminated by the false values they attacked; probably, since they were mere mortals living in the present society, they were contaminated; and so one had to keep insisting that such writers were nevertheless presenting actualities of modern experience, not merely phantoms of their neuroses.

If Bigger Thomas, as Baldwin said, "accepted a theology that denies him life," if in his Negro self-hatred he "*wants* to die because he glories in his hatred," this did not constitute a criticism of Wright unless one were prepared to assume what was simply preposterous: that Wright, for all his emotional involvement with Bigger, could not see beyond the limitations of the character he had created. This was a question Baldwin never seriously confronted in his early essays. He would describe accurately the limitations of Bigger Thomas and then, by one of those rhetorical leaps at which he is so gifted, would assume that these were also the limitations of Wright or his book.

Still another ground for Baldwin's attack was his reluctance to accept the clenched militancy of Wright's posture as both novelist and man. In a remarkable sentence appearing in "Everybody's Protest Novel," Baldwin wrote, "our humanity is our burden, our life; we need not battle for it; we need only to do what is infinitely more difficult—that is, accept it." What Baldwin was saying here was part of the outlook so many American intellectuals took over during the years of a post-war liberalism not very different from conservatism. Ralph Ellison expressed this view in terms still more extreme:

"Thus to see America with an awareness of its rich diversity and its almost magical fluidity and freedom, I was forced to conceive of a novel unburdened by the narrow naturalism which has led after so many triumphs to the final and unrelieved despair which marks so much of our current fiction." This note of willed affirmation—as if one could *decide* one's deepest and most authentic response to society!—was to be heard in many other works of the early fifties, most notably in Saul Bellow's *Adventures of Augie March*. Today it is likely to strike one as a note whistled in the dark. In response to Baldwin and Ellison, Wright would have said (I virtually quote the words he used in talking to me during the summer of 1958) that only through struggle could men with black skins, and for that matter, all the oppressed of the world, achieve their humanity. It was a lesson, said Wright with a touch of bitterness yet not without kindness, that the younger writers would have to learn in their own way and their own time. All that has happened since, bears him out.

One criticism made by Baldwin in writing about *Native Son,* perhaps because it is the least ideological, remains important. He complained that in Wright's novel "a necessary dimension has been cut away; this dimension being the relationship that Negroes bear to one another, that depth of involvement and unspoken recognition of shared experience which creates a way of life." The climate of the book, "common to most Negro protest novels . . . has led us all to believe that in Negro life there exists no tradition, no field of manners, no possibility of ritual or intercourse, such as may, for example, sustain the Jew even after he has left his father's house." It could be urged, perhaps, that in composing a novel verging on expressionism Wright need not be expected to present the Negro world with fullness, balance or nuance; but there can be little doubt that in this respect Baldwin did score a major point: the posture of militancy, no matter how great the need for it, exacts a heavy price from the writer, as indeed from everyone else. For "Even the hatred of squalor / Makes the brow grow stern / Even anger against injustice / Makes the voice grow harsh . . ." All one can ask, by way of reply, is whether the refusal to struggle may not exact a still greater price. It is a question that would soon be tormenting James Baldwin, and almost against his will. . . .

Richard Wright

by Robert A. Bone

. . . Modern art in no small measure represents an attempt to cope with the chaotic formlessness and swift flux of the modern city. Romanticism was nature-centered; it was doomed by the tons of steel and brick and asphalt which have formed a buffer between modern man and his natural environment. It was replaced by an art which is city-centered, by a realism which is the product of too many subway rides. The modern novel, like most contemporary art forms, was spawned in those vast metropolitan centers which, for better or worse, have set the tone of 20th-century life. Paris, Dublin, and Chicago have left an indelible imprint on modern fiction.

The city entered American literature at about the turn of the century, through such novels as Crane's *Maggie, a Girl of the Streets* (1891), Dreiser's *Sister Carrie* (1900), and Sinclair's *The Jungle* (1906). It was the predominantly urban themes of these "scientific naturalists," treated with an unflinching realism, which precipitated the revolt against Victorianism and gentility in American letters. For obvious reasons, Negro fiction lagged behind this development by several decades. Around 1900, when the early naturalists had already begun to probe amidst the rubbish of the city, the Negro novelist was still a hostage to Southern feudalism, along with the overwhelming bulk of the Negro population. Prior to the Great Migration, the city was not an important influence on Negro life.

Even during the 1920's when the urbanization of the Negro had progressed sufficiently to be reflected in his literature, the resulting fictional image was shallow and distorted. To the writers of the Harlem School the urban scene was symbolized more by the crowded

"*Richard Wright*" from "*Aspects of the Racial Past*" in The Negro Novel in America, *by Robert A. Bone (New Haven: Yale University Press, 1968), pp. 140–52. Copyright © 1958 by Yale University Press. Reprinted by permission of Yale University Press.*

This discussion of Wright forms part of a larger discussion of the black American novelists of the 1930s and 1940s.

cabaret than by the crowded tenement. For another decade a shallow exoticism prevented the Negro novelist from coming to grips with the hard realities of city life. It was not until the Great Depression, with its strikes and evictions, its bread lines, and its hunger marches, that the plight of the urban masses could no longer be ignored. Paradoxically, the first Negro novelist to deal with ghetto life in the Northern cities was a Southern refugee named Richard Wright.

Wright (1909–1960) was born on a plantation near Natchez, Mississippi. His father was a black peasant; his mother, a devout woman who was forced to support her family as best she could, after the desertion of her husband. Wright's childhood consisted of intermittent moves from one Southern town to the next, of part-time jobs and sporadic schooling, and of sharp lessons in what he was later to call "The Ethics of Living Jim Crow." At fifteen he struck out on his own, working in Memphis while he accumulated enough savings to go North. Arriving in Chicago on the threshold of the Great Depression, he worked at a succession of odd jobs, until his association with the Communist party lifted him to a new plane of consciousness.

From an early age Wright had dreamed of becoming a writer. In Memphis he developed a passion for reading, cutting his teeth on such authors as Dreiser, Mencken, Lewis, and Anderson. "All my life," he writes in *Black Boy*, "had shaped me for the realism, the naturalism of the modern novel." A long apprenticeship ensued, however, before Wright was to attempt a full-length novel. His first published pieces were poems, articles, and stories, written for what may loosely be termed the Communist party press. While Wright was employed on the Federal Writers' Project, *American Stuff* carried one of his stories, which resulted in the publication of his first book, *Uncle Tom's Children* (1936). These five novellas of anguish and violence clearly reveal the strength of Wright's emotional ties to the deep South. His other major publications include a novel (*Native Son*, 1940), a pictorial history (*Twelve Million Black Voices*, 1941), an autobiography (*Black Boy*, 1945), and a posthumous collection of stories (*Eight Men*, 1961).[1] Richard Wright's *Native Son* marks a high point in the history of the Negro novel, not only because it is a work of art in its own right but

---

[1] In 1953 Wright published a second novel, *The Outsider*, a work strongly influenced by French existentialism and far inferior to *Native Son*. This was followed in 1958 by *The Long Dream*, a still more disastrous performance.

because it influenced a whole generation of Negro novelists. To the average well-read American, and not without justice, *Native Son* is the most familiar novel—and Bigger Thomas the most memorable character—in Negro fiction. The book was an instantaneous popular success, and as a result Wright became the first fully professional Negro novelist. A best-seller and Book-of-the-Month Club selection, *Native Son* was successfully adapted to the Broadway stage by Orson Welles and was later revived as a movie by Wright himself. Since its appearance in 1940, the novel has inspired a host of imitators who may be said to constitute the Wright School of postwar Negro fiction.

By way of preliminary remarks, three important influences on *Native Son* should be considered. In terms of literary lineage the novel derives from the early American naturalists, by way of Dos Passos, Farrell, Steinbeck, and the late Dreiser. *An American Tragedy* (1925) in particular seems to have been a model for *Native Son*. Both novels make use of criminality as their chief dramatic device, and in each case the crime is the natural and inevitable product of a warped society. Both authors draw the data for their trial scenes, in classic naturalist fashion, from authentic court records: Dreiser from a murder case in upstate New York, and Wright from the famous Leopold and Loeb kidnap-murder in Chicago. Both novels, through their titles, make the point that Clyde Griffiths and Bigger Thomas are native American products, and not, as Wright remarks, imported from Moscow or anywhere else. Both authors advance a guilt-of-the-nation thesis as a corollary to their environmentalist view of crime.

Much of the raw material for *Native Son* was provided by Wright's personal experience in metropolitan Chicago. For several hard-pressed years he worked at all kinds of jobs, from porter and dishwasher to ditch-digger and post office clerk. One job as agent for a burial society took him inside the south-side tenement houses, where he saw the corrosive effects of ghetto life on the Negro migrant. During the depression a relief agency placed him in the South Side Boys' Club, where he met the live models from whom he was to sketch Bigger Thomas: "They were a wild and homeless lot, culturally lost, spiritually disinherited, candidates for the clinics, morgues, prisons, reformatories, and the electric chair of the state's death house." [2] Meanwhile, even as his empirical knowledge

[2] Richard Wright, "I Tried to Be a Communist," *Atlantic Monthly, 174* (Aug. 1944), p. 68.

of urban life increased, Wright was introduced to the theoretical
concepts of Marxism through the John Reed Club and the Communist party.

Wright joined the party in 1934, breaking decisively about ten
years later. The extent of his involvement has been, to put it as
kindly as possible, modestly understated in *The God That Failed*
(1949). For several years, Wright acted as a dependable wheel
horse in a wide variety of party activities. To his credit, however, a
stubborn and uncorruptible individualism kept him in constant
conflict with the party bureaucracy, leading eventually to his break
and expulsion. Of his main motive for joining the party Wright has
written in retrospect: "[The party] did not say 'Be like us and we
will like you, maybe.' It said: 'If you possess enough courage to
speak out what you are, you will find that you are not alone.' " [3] As
an excluded Negro and an alienated intellectual, Wright needed
above all to feel this sense of belonging. That he was able to find it,
however fleetingly, only within the ranks of the Communist party
is a commentary on the failure of the democratic left.

Wright's debt to Marxism is quite a different matter from his
personal history in the Communist party. The party, it must be
understood, manipulates Marxism for its own ends, which are the
ends of the Russian ruling class. Yet the basic ideas of Karl Marx,
like those of Sigmund Freud, are capable of effecting so vast a revolution in the consciousness of an individual that he may never
recapture his former state of innocence. For Richard Wright, Marxism became a way of ordering his experience; it became, in literary
terms, his unifying mythos. It provided him with a means of interpreting the urban scene which the Harlem School had lacked. Above
all, it provided him with an intellectual framework for understanding his life as a Negro.

Wright, more than any Negro author who preceded him, has a
sense of the presentness of his racial past. This sense of history,
which was part and parcel of his Marxist outlook, has been recorded in *Twelve Million Black Voices* (1941), published hard on
the heels of *Native Son*. In this folk history of the American Negro,
Wright sees the black ghetto as the end product of a long historical
process (p. 93):

> Perhaps never in history has a more utterly unprepared folk wanted
> to go to the city; we were barely born as a folk when we headed

[3] *Ibid.*, p. 62.

for the tall and sprawling centers of steel and stone. We who were landless on the land; we who had barely managed to live in family groups; we who needed the ritual and guidance of established institutions to hold our atomized lives together in lines of purpose . . . we who had had our personalities blasted with 200 years of slavery had been turned loose to shift for ourselves.

It was in this perspective that Wright saw the life of Bigger Thomas.

The most impressive feature of *Native Son* is its narrative drive. From the outset the novel assumes a fierce pace which carries the reader breathlessly through Bigger's criminal career. Wright allows as little interruption of the action as possible, with no chapter divisions as such and only an occasional break to mark a swift transition or change of scene. At the same time, he writes with great economy, breaking with the comprehensive and discursive tradition of the naturalistic novel. He provides only three brief glimpses of Bigger's life prior to the main action of the novel: his relationship with his family, with his gang, and with his girl, Bessie. The reader must supply the rest, for Wright's presentation is not direct but metaphorical.

On a literal level *Native Son* consists of three Books, dealing with a murder, a flight and capture, and a trial. But the murder and the circumstances which surround it are in reality an extended metaphor, like the whale hunt in *Moby Dick*. The novel is not to be read merely as the story of a gruesome crime, though it is that. It is the hidden meaning of Bigger's life, as revealed by the murder, which is the real subject of *Native Son*. The novel is a modern epic, consisting of action on the grand scale. As such, it functions as a commentary on the more prosaic plane of daily living.

Book I is called "Fear." Its structure pulsates in mounting waves of violence, beginning with the opening rat scene, increasing during Bigger's fight with Gus, and culminating in murder. Each successive wave of violence is a means of reducing fear, for great fear automatically produces great violence in Bigger. He has been so conditioned that being found in a white girl's room is the ultimate fear-inspiring situation. When the blind Mrs. Dalton appears as a white blur in the doorway of Mary's room, Bigger is seized with hysterical terror, and he murders. It is both an accident and not an accident, for the first characteristic of Bigger's life which the murder reveals is his uncontrollable fear of whites.

The second aspect of Bigger's normal life to receive thematic stress is his bitter sense of deprivation: "We black and they white.

They got things and we ain't. They do things and we can't. It's just like living in jail. Half the time I feel like I'm on the outside of the world peeping in through a knot-hole in the fence" (p. 17).[4] Living on the margin of his culture, Bigger is constantly tormented by the glitter of the dominant civilization. "The Gay Woman," a movie which he watches while waiting to rob a neighborhood store, is emblematic of that world of cocktail parties, golf, and spinning roulette wheels from which he is forever excluded. To fill the intolerable void in his life he seeks "something big"—the "job" at Blum's which never comes off, his real job as chauffeur and handyman for the Daltons. He finally breaks through the confines of his daily life by committing murder.

Book II, "Flight," opens with a recapitulation of Bigger's relations with family and gang, to show how they have changed as a result of the murder. Bigger has now achieved heroic stature: "He had murdered and created a new life for himself." This is the dominant irony of Book II—that Bigger finds fulfillment only by the most violent defiance of the legal and moral precepts of the society which oppresses him. As a criminal, Bigger achieves a sense of purpose, a feeling of elation which is a measure of the meaninglessness of his former existence.

After the fact of Bigger's rebirth is established, the narrative proceeds with a series of interrogations by Peggy, by the Daltons, and finally by the police. Bigger's conduct throughout is determined by the heightened perceptions which he enjoys as a result of the murder: "The whole thing came to him in the form of a powerful and simple feeling; there was in everyone a great hunger to believe that made him blind, and if he could see while others were blind, then he could get what he wanted and never be caught at it" (p. 91). Bigger learns to exploit the blindness of others, "fooling the white folks" during his interrogation, and this is again something deep in his racial heritage, springing from a long tradition of telling whites whatever they want to hear.

At last comes discovery, flight, and capture. Once again the action of the novel serves as an oblique comment on Bigger's "normal" way of life: "But it was familiar, this running away. All his life he had been knowing that sooner or later something like this would come to him" (p. 187). No such fear-ridden sequence as Bigger's flight and capture is possible without a proportionate act of violence. Bessie's

---

[4] [Page references here are to the first edition of *Native Son* (Harper and Row, 1940).—Ed.]

murder, compounding horror upon grisly horror, serves to dispel any lingering doubt concerning Bigger's guilt. Learning from Dreiser's mistake, Wright takes no chances that his audience may be diverted from his main point by quibbling over the "accidental" nature of Mary Dalton's death. At the same time, the audience knows intuitively that it is Mary's murder, and not Bessie's, for which society will demand Bigger's life.

The successful fusion of narrative and metaphorical levels in *Native Son* is only a sample of Wright's craftsmanship. Not the least of his problems is to induce his readers to identify with Bigger in spite of his monstrous crimes. This he accomplishes by a tone which subtly controls and defines the reader's attitude toward Bigger. It is a tone of anguish and despair, established at the outset by Wright's epigraph from the Book of Job: "Even today is my complaint rebellious; my stroke is heavier than my groaning." Thus the stark horror of *Native Son* is balanced by the spiritual anguish which, in a sense, produced it. This note of anguish, which emphasizes Bigger's suffering, is so intense as to be almost physical in character. It is sustained by a style which can only be called visceral. The author writes from his guts, describing the emotional state of his characters in graphic psychosomatic terms. It is a characteristic device which has its source in Wright's aching memory of the deep South.

Notwithstanding Wright's professed naturalism, the symbolic texture of *Native Son* is exceptionally rich. The whole novel is contained in the first few pages when Bigger, in unconscious anticipation of his own fate, corners a huge black rat and kills him with a skillet. Much of Wright's meaning is conveyed by appropriate "objective correlatives" for Bigger's inner feelings and emotions. The icy gales and heavy snowfalls of Books I and II represent a hostile white environment: "To Bigger and his kind white people were not really people; they were a sort of great natural force, like a stormy sky looming overhead" (p. 97). Throughout Book II the red glow of the furnace appears as a projection of Bigger's guilt. A series of breathing and choking images anticipates the manner of the murder, linking it symbolically to Bigger's choked and stifled life. There is a constant play on blindness, focused around the figure of Mrs. Dalton but aimed ultimately at the reader, who is expected to grope his way to an understanding of Bigger's life.

A lesser artist would have directed Bigger's symbolic revolt against a brutal oppressor, but Wright understands that such an approach would only make his audience feel smug and superior. He chooses as Bigger's victim a girl who is "friendly to Negroes," but whose kindness under the circumstances is a bitter mockery. By this device, Wright means to suggest that Bigger's sickness is too deep to be reached by kindness, and at the same time to involve his audience in responsibility for Bigger's crime. The Daltons, who are people of good will, hire Bigger because they "want to give Negroes a chance." But they also own real estate on the South Side, and have thus helped to make the black ghetto what it is. They are, in short, just as innocent and just as guilty as we.

Book I portrays the old Bigger; Book II, the new; Book III, the Bigger who might have been. The bare narrative is concerned with Bigger's fight for his life, but the dramatic tension of Book III is centered elsewhere. The important question is not whether Bigger will be spared, but whether he will be saved. Bigger's impending death in the electric chair is simply the crisis which forces a resolution of his inner conflict, thus revealing what is basic in his personality. After his talk with the lawyer, Max—the most intimate of his life—Bigger feels that he must make a decision: "In order to walk to that chair he had to weave his feelings into a hard shield of either hope or hate. To fall between them would mean living and dying in a fog of fear" (p. 305). On what terms will Bigger die; in hope or in hate? This is the tension of Book III.

Bigger's basic problem is to find someone or something he can trust. Kardiner and Livesey have written of the lower-class Negro family: "The result of the continuous frustration in childhood is to create a personality devoid of confidence in human relations, of an eternal vigilance and distrust of others. This is a purely defensive maneuver, which purports to protect the individual against the repeatedly traumatic effects of disappointment and frustration. He must operate on the assumption that the world is hostile." [5] This lack of relatedness appears above all in Bigger's relationship with Bessie. As Max points out, "His relationship to this poor black girl reveals his relationship to the world." It is a mutually exploitative affair, devoid of devotion, loyalty, or trust—luxuries which are denied to Bigger and Bessie by the circumstances of their lives.

Bigger's lack of relatedness is presented symbolically at the end of Book II, just before his capture: "Under it all some part of his mind was beginning to stand aside; he was going behind his curtain, his wall, looking out with sullen stares of contempt." This retreat,

---

[5] Abram Kardiner and Lionel Livesey, *The Mark of Oppression* (New York, Norton, 1951), p. 308.

amounting almost to a catatonic trance, sets the stage for the dominant conflict in Book III. As Bigger slowly awakens from his trance, his fierce life-drive, set off perfectly by the death cell which he occupies, struggles toward some sort of relatedness with his fellows: "If he reached out his hands, and if his hands were electric wires, and if his heart were a battery giving life and fire to those hands, and if he reached out with his hands and touched other people, if he did that, would there be a reply, a shock?" (p. 307).

The structure of Book III is essentially a series of attempts by Bigger to realize this vision. He seeks desperately for a basis for hope but discards one alternative after another. He rejects his family ("Go home, Ma"); his fellow prisoners ("Are you the guy who pulled the Dalton job?"); the race leaders ("they almost like white folks when it comes to guys like me"); and religion. The old preacher tempts Bigger with the Christian explanation of suffering, but when the mob burns a fiery cross outside the jail, the cross of love turns to a cross of hate. Bigger finds it hardest to reject Jan and Max. These are the last symbols of relatedness to which he clings, and the main conflict of the novel occurs between them and Bigger's deepest experience as a Negro—his distrust of whites, his Negro nationalism.

Bigger's relations with Jan and Max cannot be understood apart from the context of Wright's experience in the Communist party. Most Negro Communists—and Wright was no exception—are Negro nationalists, for it is precisely the most embittered, antiwhite Negroes to whom the party offers the possibility of revenge. But the vast majority of American Communists, after all, are white. Paradoxically, the most white-hating Negro is thrust, by his membership in the party, into what is surely, whatever else it may be, one of the freest arenas of interracial contact in America. The result is an agonizing psychological conflict, as the Negro nationalist, newly won to Communism, struggles to relate to his white comrades. This is the conflict which is bothering Wright in Book III of *Native Son,* expressed on a somewhat primitive level through Bigger's relations with the white Communists, Jan and Max.

To Bigger, Communism is a matter not of ideology but of relatedness. Jan and Max are the flimsy base on which he tries to erect his shield of hope. Jan, through an act of understanding and forgiveness, evokes what is almost a religious response from Bigger, where the old colored preacher had failed: "The word had become flesh. For the first time in his life a white man became a human being to him."

The resolution of the novel, however, comes in terms of Bigger's relationship with Max. Max serves as Bigger's father confessor as well as his lawyer, and Bigger comes closest to establishing a human contact with him.

After Max's speech fails, and after all avenues have been closed to Bigger, Max makes a final visit to Bigger's cell. Bigger seeks to recapture their former intimacy, but Max is too concerned with comforting him in the face of death. Max then tries to communicate his vision of Communism to Bigger, but fails. As his shield of hope slips from his grasp, Bigger takes up the shield of hate which is his destiny. The impact comes through Max's reactions: "Bigger saw Max back away from him with compressed lips. . . . Max lifted his hand to touch Bigger, but did not. . . . Max's eyes were full of terror. . . . He felt for the door, keeping his face averted. . . . He did not turn around. . . . Max paused, but did not look" (pp. 358–59). What terrifies Max is that Bigger, re-possessed by hate, ends by accepting what life has made him: a killer. Bigger's real tragedy is not that he dies, but that he dies in hatred. A tragic figure, he struggles for love and trust against a hostile environment which defeats him in the end.

Book III, and therefore the novel, suffers from a major structural flaw, flowing from the fact that Wright has failed to digest Communism artistically. The Communist party is simply not strong enough as a symbol of relatedness; Bigger's hatred, firmly anchored in his Negro nationalism, is hardly challenged. The contest is unequal, because there is nothing in Bigger's life that corresponds to "Communism." As a result, the conflict between love and hate, between universal brotherhood and Negro nationalism, cannot be successfully internalized. Wright is forced to go outside of Bigger, to Jan and Max, both of whom are more the mouthpieces for a thesis than credible characters in their own right. Wright is sure of Bigger, but Jan and Max elude him. In noting his failure to realize Communism artistically, it is not irrelevant to recall that for Wright himself, the party was no shield of hope.

Since Bigger is unable to bear the weight of political symbolism intended for him, Wright is forced to resort to rhetoric. The first two books of *Native Son* contain two levels of meaning; the bare action, and a running account of Bigger's feelings at the time. Now a third level is introduced: an interpretation of the action, undertaken by the author through the medium of Max's speech. This speech, with its guilt-of-the-nation thesis, throws the novel badly out of focus. The reader is likely to come away thinking that Bigger committed a horrible crime to which he was driven by a still more horrible environment, which I, the reader, have helped to create. Fictionally, however, the novel makes a different point: Bigger is a human being whose environment has made him incapable of relating meaningfully to other human beings except through murder.

Not satisfied with interpreting his own novel through Max, Wright tries again in his article "How Bigger Was Born": "Bigger, an American product, a native son of this land, carries within him the potentialities of either fascism or communism." [6] But Wright can only attempt in retrospect to impose a political symbolism on the novel which he fails to realize fictionally. He simply cannot fit the ideas of Bigger into those of the Communist party. A white Bigger could be a fascist; a colored Bigger with trade-union experience could be a Communist. But Bigger is a Negro without fellow workers and is therefore only Bigger, a memorable figure in contemporary literature whom Wright created in spite of his own political ideology.

Of the Negro novelists who wrote during the Great Depression, Richard Wright came closest to expressing the essential spirit of the decade. At bottom, the Depression years witnessed a continuation of the cultural dualism of the Negro Renaissance. During the thirties the Negro novelist maintained an active interest in his Negro heritage, systematically exploring the racial past in his search for distinctive literary material. Upon this base, in accordance with the climate of the times, was superimposed the formula of "proletarian art." Wright's contribution to the Negro novel was precisely his fusion of a pronounced racialism with a broader tradition of social protest.

The Red Decade was brought to an abrupt close by America's entry into World War II. As the unemployed workers were gradually absorbed into war industry, and as New Dealers and Communists alike raised the slogan of "national unity," the radicalism of the thirties faded into oblivion. The intelligentsia's brief excursion into proletarian art was over. During the war years, in any case, literary activity became a luxury and like so many aspects of the national life was laid aside for the duration. The Negro novel entered a period of wartime quiescence, from which it emerged into a vastly altered postwar world.

[6] *Saturday Review*, 22 (1940), 1–4, 17–20.

The Bad Nigger

by Dan McCall

. . . Yet Wright himself was well aware of the danger he was running. In "How Bigger Was Born" he shows how deeply he knew that such a book could "revitalize prejudices and projections on both sides" (Solotaroff) and "reinforce the American guilt and fear" (Baldwin). Wright asked himself: "What will white people think if I draw the picture of such a Negro boy? Will they not at once say: 'See, didn't we tell you all along that niggers are like that? Now, look, one of their own kind has come along and drawn the picture for us!' " Wright presents the various objections from all sides, then finally turns them down. Or, rather, Bigger himself turns them down: "Bigger won over all these claims; he won because I felt that I was hunting on the trail of more exciting and thrilling game." *Native Son,* then, would be a big-game hunt, Wright would go out on imaginative safari for the man-eater, the "beast in the skull," try to find him and kill him first.

Wright provides us with artistic and moral equipment to understand that hunt as more than an outraged repetition of a stereotype. Of key importance is that sense of psychodrama, that the surface reality is a way of getting to a psychic reality. These things are true *in the head,* in the mind of history. Each of the three times Bigger kills he goes for the head. In the first scene, when he throws the skillet at the rat, he is "cursing hysterically" while he crushes its skull. Mary he smothers, a pillow over her head, and then in the basement he beheads her. And when he kills Bessie in the abandoned apartment building he pounds time after time at

---

From "The Bad Nigger" in The Example of Richard Wright, *by Dan McCall (New York: Harcourt Brace Jovanovich, Inc., 1969), pp. 74–85. Copyright © 1969 by Dan McCall. Reprinted by permission of Harcourt Brace Jovanovich, Inc.*

The complete essay traces Wright's relationship to the naturalistic and Gothic traditions of white American literature and explores Native Son's *technical flaws and the ultimate futility of Bigger's rage.*

her head with the brick. His terror and hate of the head comes home to him in one of his nightmares:

> He had a big package in his arms so wet and slippery and heavy that he could scarcely hold onto it and he wanted to know what was in the package and he stopped near an alley corner and un-wrapped it and the paper fell away and he saw—it was his *own* head—his own head lying with black face and half-closed eyes. . . .

Throughout, the physical description that Wright rushes by us makes us feel the emotional force of the objects but not see them with any real accuracy: we are aware of the furnace and storm as poles of the imagination—fire and ice—in a world of symbolic presences. Continually the world is transformed into a kind of massive skull, and the people are figments of that skull's imagination. Hawthorne's Pyncheon house was an asymmetrical, grotesque image of the Pyncheon sensibility; just as Poe's house [*sic*] of Usher had its great central crack that would make it "Fall," the schizophrenia that finally splits and kills Roderick Usher. In *Native Son* Bigger sees the houses of the black ghetto as great heads. With Bessie he sees a "snow-covered building whose many windows gaped blackly, like the eye-sockets of empty skulls." And when Bigger lives alone and terrified in the skull of one of those buildings he is playing out his role, consistently symbolized throughout the book, as an occupant of our imagination, a man imprisoned in our minds. Wherever he turns, trying to break open heads, he wants to get out of the mental cage. Wright's insistence on the image presents the violence as an act of the imagination, turning to the terms of its imprisonment, and insistently reminding us, through those key terms, that what is going on here is a psychic struggle, an act of imaginative liberation.

All of which says, finally, that *Native Son* is no more a Gothic romance than it is a naturalistic novel. The Gothic romance involves a complicated relationship between the creative imagination and the external world and establishes a distance between them which *Native Son* simply does not, in any formal way, observe. Hawthorne goes back, in his greatest success, two hundred years; we participate in his imaginative recapturing of the past. There is a certain stability in Hawthorne's sense of that past and a certain assurance in his setting up of the key signs and interpreting them. Poe creates extremities of consciousness, aberrations, but only while showing us that that is what they are. He makes his extremes on his own terms. In both Hawthorne and Poe we have the sense of a conscious manipulation of the materials, a willful departure from actuality and a distortion of it to get back to the truth that actuality had hidden from us.

Wright had no possibility of any settled distance; the willful distortions of Hawthorne and Poe were forced upon Wright by the dominant culture. One of the reasons Wright could not fashion a Gothic romance was most clearly stated by Wright himself in the last sentence of his essay "How Bigger Was Born." All through that final paragraph Wright talks of James and Hawthorne and Poe, their relationship to the American scene, and then concludes that paragraph and his essay with a perception that shows us more clearly than anything else how his problem was different from theirs: "And if Poe were alive, he would not have to invent horror; horror would invent him." The nineteenth-century writers could erect fantasies in the head; Wright was trying to rid himself of the fantasy in his.

In "Bright and Morning Star" the final scene is one of unbearable horror; the old Negro mother keeps begging the white men to shoot her son so he won't suffer, but they only break his legs over a log, crunching the kneecaps with a crowbar, and then split his eardrums, "his eyes showing white amazement in a world without sound." That last phrase recurs in *Native Son* not in a scene of a black man being mutilated but in a scene where a black man remembers how he mutilated a white woman: suddenly the winter fields around Bigger burst into "a world of magic whiteness without sound." The change is from the black man being killed to the black man killing. Similarly, after the imagined sexual transgression, the whites of "Big Boy Leaves Home" mutilate and burn the Negro boy; in *Native Son,* after the fear that he will be accused of sexual transgression, the black boy mutilates and burns the white body. In this way the sales figures of *Native Son* are not so surprising; it is a book that the whites already know about, the story of their guilt, but it is a shocking new report from the other side of their own wall.

A stereotype is not an archetype. *Native Son* leads us into myth, taking a common assumption of the culture and elaborating it in so accurate and energetic a way that the culture finds in it the expression of one of its deepest drives. Bigger Thomas is a legendary figure of the Western mind, belonging with figures like Robinson Crusoe, Bigger embodying as successfully the Myth of Race as Crusoe embodies the Myth of Individual Enterprise. James Baldwin's struggle with Bigger is an intensely moving one to watch; while Baldwin cannot relax his rage, he is far too intelligent to let anyone bully him into false terms. Yet I think the answer to his repeated objection (that Wright only reinforces stereotypes and repeats them in fury) will have to come from the fact, simply, that no white man could have written *Native Son*. The extraordinary quality of the book is its "niggerness." Here the black man is struggling to release himself by beating the white man at his own game. Wright may not be able to write the romance, but in many ways he is like Hester Prynne in Hawthorne's most famous one: cast out of the community, branded with a terrible letter (skin) of shame, he wears it proudly. Hester's embroidery of her symbol and Wright's assertion of his Biggerness is a way of wearing proudly the shame the culture lays down; it is a way of taking the terms and fighting back. Wright could not assert *Négritude*, for it was not historically available; he could assert his niggerhood, and he could do it in such a way that the stereotype would be lifted into myth.

Wright said that finally his choice to write the book came when he decided, "I must write this novel, not only for others to read, but to free *myself* of this sense of shame and fear. In fact, the novel, as time passed, grew upon me to the extent that it became a necessity to write it; the writing of it turned into a way of living for me." Wright was creating and living every day with his beast in the skull, Bigger, the psychopath. Norman Mailer has written in "The White Negro" that:

> Many people with a psychoanalytical orientation often confuse the psychopath with the psychotic. Yet the terms are polar. The psychotic is legally insane, the psychopath is not; the psychotic is almost always incapable of discharging in physical acts the rage of his frustration, while the psychopath at his extreme is virtually as incapable of restraining his violence.

And the creation of Bigger Thomas, for Richard Wright, was to get at the psychopath in himself, his twisted roots and frantic edges. Mailer goes on in his famous essay to suggest that such an artist must go "exploring backward along the road" of all the rape and robbery and murder, all the real or potential crimes, in order "to find those violent parallels to the violent and often hopeless contradictions he knew as an infant and as a child . . . and so free himself to remake a bit of his nervous system." Wright was, as his anguished statements in "How Bigger Was Born" make clear, engaged in just this task. Exorcism. Which is not at all merely to repeat a stereotype but a way of exploring the empirical truths of the passions that sustain the stereotype. A stereotype could not exist if it did not have something to do with the truth; if the stereotype does not offer some accuracy about a people or the way we feel about a people, it would cease to have imaginative currency. Further, the stereotype separates a man from himself. A man cannot find himself because the stereotype interferes by insisting that his category is more than his individuality. In *Native Son* Wright attempts to destroy the cliché by giving it its full imaginative due.

He would say in "I Bite the Hand That Feeds Me" (*Atlantic,* June 1940), "I wrote *Native Son* to show what manner of men and women our 'society of the majority' breeds, and my aim was to depict a character in terms of the living tissue and texture of daily consciousness." In that way, because he was able to do that, he was able to give white Americans the bad nigger—whom they knew— but he was also able to give those readers Bigger Thomas—whom they did not know. However desperate, it is an act of creation. In *The Wretched of the Earth* Fanon advised the militant black intellectual that sometimes he would have to "will to be a nigger, not just a nigger like all other niggers but a real nigger, a Negro cur, just the sort of nigger the white man wants. . . ." Someone, say, like Bigger Thomas. Richard Wright, so contemptuous of those "prim and decorous Ambassadors" in assimilationist Negro literature, was pulling out of himself and pushing onto the page "just the sort of nigger the white man wants." For centuries the white community had been standing on top of the world shouting down into the cave, "We know you're down there, we know you're down there." Small wonder the white world shrank back when the growl came up:

"Ah, but I am."

In his essay on Bigger's birth, Wright said that "life had made the plot over and over again, to the extent that I knew it by heart." Repeatedly he had seen black boys picked off the streets to be charged with an unsolved case of "rape." "This thing happens so often that to my mind it had become a representative symbol of the Negro's uncertain position in America." Robert Nixon was apprehended and sent sprawling across the front page of the *Tribune* while Wright was in mid-passage with Bigger Thomas. The actual case is a part of history—as the novel is part of the literary history—of the thing itself. In Chicago in 1938 two black men were testifying to the myth, one with a brick and the other with a book.

Richard, like Bigger, lived in a Chicago slum with his mother. As an insurance agent Wright had visited various black kitchenettes like the one with which his book would begin. In the opening scene the people driven so closely together are driven violently apart. Wright would say the following year, in *12 Million Black Voices,* "The kitchenette throws desperate and unhappy people into an unbearable closeness of association, thereby increasing latent friction, giving birth to never-ending quarrels of recrimination, accusation, and vindictiveness, producing warped personalities." The full recognition of how the "kitchenette" (which refers to the cramped apartment itself, not just the cooking area) forms Bigger's sensibility—or how it deprived him of what we could call a "sensibility"—was one of Wright's most daring and significant choices.

In "Many Thousands Gone," Baldwin saw that "Bigger has no discernible relationship to himself, to his own life, to his own people, nor to any other people" and because of that "a necessary dimension has been cut away." But that was surely Wright's point; he knew that he was cutting away a dimension. He said in "How Bigger Was Born" that he planned for his black boy to be "estranged from the religion and the folk culture of his race"—a statement that shows that Wright was consciously pulling things away and not, as the criticism against Wright might lead one to believe, that Wright just didn't know how to show them. In *12 Million Black Voices* he summarized:

> Perhaps never in history has a more utterly unprepared folk wanted to go to the city: we were barely born as a folk when we headed for the tall and sprawling centers of steel and stone. We, who were landless on the land; we, who had barely managed to live in family groups; we, who needed the ritual and guidance of institutions to hold our atomized lives together in lines of purpose; we, who had known only relationships to people and not relationships to things; we, who had never belonged to any organizations except the church and burial societies; we, who had had our personalities blasted with two hundred years of slavery and had been turned loose to shift for ourselves. . . .

In the figure of Bigger Thomas, Wright was trying to show the ultimate sense of horror: unpreparedness set loose in a metropolis.

Bigger has nothing to hold him back and nothing to define his responses other than the blackness of his skin. He is, as his mother wails, "black crazy"; his mind is crazed by his color. He is incapable of a nonracial thought. His obsession produces what Wright would later call, "The State of Exaggeration." In *White Man, Listen!*, Wright says that "one of the aspects of life of the American Negro that has amazed observers is the emotional intensity with which he attacks ordinary, daily problems." How can the mind ever relax or grow when its defining problem is always and unbearably one thing? Wright offers as an example the problem a Negro has in renting a place to live; the overriding question, the one that gathers all the usual questions of whether the place is clean, whether it is well-made, whether it's near a school, whether it's near stores, is only one question: can a black person live there? And as the great migration moved northward in the twenties and thirties the black folk found their answer. They would live in the kitchenette.

This "state of exaggeration" that Wright speaks of is most clearly seen in the kitchenette by an overwhelming fear of being looked at. The kitchenette means lack of privacy. On the first page of *Native Son,* when people get out of bed, the first words are "Turn your heads so I can dress." Day after day in the ghetto that is the call to society; and on the second day of Wright's story, in the center section of his book, Vera repeats the line "Turn your head so I can dress." Even when one is dressed, the fear continues at the breakfast table, this horror of being seen.

> "Stop looking at me, Bigger!"
> "Aw, shut up and eat your breakfast!"
> "Ma, make 'im stop looking at me!"
> "I ain't looking at her, Ma!"
> "You *is!*" Vera said.

And so it goes, on into the night where children are given their sexual education because the mother and father cannot not give it to them. After his murders Bigger roams the ghetto apartment houses, climbing them and peering into windows where he sees

> through a window without shades . . . a room in which were two small iron beds with sheets dirty and crumpled. In one bed sat three naked black children looking across the room to the other bed on which lay a man and woman, both naked and black. . . . There were quick, jerky movements on the bed where the man and woman lay, and the three children were watching.

Bigger sees it as a memory, for he, too, had often "awakened and watched his father and mother." He climbs on up with one last look in at "the man and woman moving jerkily in tight embrace, and the three children watching."

Wright's point is not to deny the Negro's "folk culture." He was trying to show that for these urban slum dwellers the folk culture was swallowed in unbearable closeness. This emptiness and fear of being looked at Bigger carries with him all the day long. The scene which begins the book is present at the very center of the crime where Bigger is hysterical at not being able to get the full human form into a tight place. He has to cut off the head. Bigger's head, his sensibility, was cut off in the kitchenette. (And the severed head appears in his dream as his own.) At the end of the book Max keeps asking Bigger what Mary Dalton had done to him that made Bigger say, "I ain't sorry she's dead." Bigger struggles for the answer; all he knows is that he hated her. He stammers and tries to find it and then vaguely he gets an image of his sister

> Vera, sitting on the edge of a chair crying because he had shamed her by "looking" at her; he saw her rise and fling her shoe at him. He shook his head confused.

That is it: racial misery is indecent exposure.

And so Wright would tell us at the beginning of his story that Bigger's relationship to his family was that "he lived with them, but behind a wall, a curtain." When he relates to black people he takes his violence out on them. His hate bottles up and has to get out; since it cannot reach its stimulus, the white man, it is expelled on blacks. He corners his pal, Gus, and holds a knife blade at his mouth, saying, "Lick it." What he wants to do, of course, is hold it at the white man's lips, draw blood from the white man's tongue. But he can't get at him. Bigger "had heard it said that white people felt it was good when one Negro killed another; it meant that they had one Negro less to contend with." When a Negro says he is afraid to go to Mississippi because "down there they'd as soon kill you as look at you" he does not refer merely to the white race. Bigger cannot feel "guilt" about his murders. His is a mind in which "guilt" plays as negligible a part as it did in the whites who set fire to Bobo. Bigger cannot say, "I have killed a *human being*," for there are no human beings on his planet. Bessie was not at all his "sweetheart," only the "girl" he had because other boys had them. His relationship to her is his relationship to the black community;

he will use and enjoy her when he can and strike out when she gets in his way. "The black girl was merely 'evidence.' And under it all he knew that the white people did not really care about Bessie's being killed."

Bigger is, then, one of the Negro's "roles" (in spite of the continuing objection that he is not), and the white reader can see it more clearly now as black voices from the ghetto begin to come out with verification of how accurate Bigger was. Anyone who has read *The Autobiography of Malcolm X* or *Manchild in the Promised Land* or Eldridge Cleaver's remarkable *Soul on Ice* can see Biggers in the characters the authors draw around them and explore, with considerable courage, in themselves. Wright does not, as Baldwin said, "cut a necessary dimension away." Again, white America beat him to it. Had Wright not portrayed Bigger in this way he would have been cutting a "necessary dimension away" not from his figure but from the importance of the forces that would make him what he was. To create a "folk tradition" in the slum—that is, to create whole human beings in a brutally fragmented world—would not be to take that world seriously. It would be a gross underestimation of how massive the damage is. Wright saw that if people do not have any chance to get culture it is rather unlikely that they will have its blessings. . . .

Richard Wright: Blackness and the
Adventure of Western Culture

by George E. Kent

. . . *Lawd Today* enlarges our perspective on *Native Son,* for it creates the universe of Bigger Thomas in terms more dense than the carefully chosen symbolic reference points of *Native Son.* The continuity of Wright's concerns stand out with great clarity and depth. Running through all Wright's works and thoroughly pervading his personality is his identification with and rejection of the West, and his identification with and rejection of the conditions of black life. *Lawd Today* is primarily concerned with the latter.

In *Native Son,* Wright's greatest work, he returned to the rebel outsider, the character with revolutionary will and the grit to make existential choices. Bigger Thomas, like the heroic characters of *Uncle Tom's Children* finally insists upon defining the meaning of his life: ". . . What I killed for, I am," cries Bigger at the end of his violent and bloody life.

Wright early establishes the myth of the heritage of Man, Western Man, as a counterpoint to the disinherited condition of Bigger Thomas, a Southern black migrant with an eighth grade education. In the first section of the novel, Bigger expresses his frustration by violent and cowardly reactions, and by references to the rituals of power and freedom that he envies. What does he wish to happen, since he complains that nothing happens in his universe? " 'Anything,' Bigger said with a wide sweep of his dingy palm, a sweep that included all the possible activities of the world."

"Richard Wright: Blackness and the Adventure of Western Culture" by George E. Kent. From CLA Journal, XII (June, 1969), 339–43. Copyright © 1969 by College Language Association. Reprinted by permission of the author and The College Language Association.

The original essay traces the presence of what W. E. B. DuBois (The Souls of Black Folk, 1903) called the "double consciousness" of the black American in Wright's works.

Then their eyes [Bigger's and his gang's] were riveted; a slate-
colored pigeon swooped down to the middle of the steel car tracks
and began strutting to and fro with ruffled feathers, its fat neck
bobbing with regal pride. A street car rumbled forward and the
pigeon rose swiftly through the air on wings stretched so taut and
sheer that Bigger could see the god of the sun through their trans-
lucent tips. He tilted his head and watched the slate-colored bird
flap and wheel out of sight over the ridge of a high roof.
"Now, if I could only do that," Bigger said.[1]

Bigger, himself, instinctively realizes that a job and night school
will not fundamentally alter his relationship to the universe. To
the white and wealthy Mrs. Dalton's query concerning night school,
his mind silently makes a vague response: "Night school was all
right, but he had other plans. Well, he didn't know just what they
were right now, but he was working them out." [2] As to the job with
the Daltons, it is but an extension of the System that holds him in
contempt and stifles his being; the "relief" people will cut off his
food and starve his family if he does not take it. Because of the resulting pressure from his family for physical comfort and survival,
". . . he felt that they had tricked him into a cheap surrender."
The job and night school would have programmed his life into con-
formity with what Wright called the "pet nigger system," [3] but
would not have gained respect for his manhood.

Bigger Thomas and Richard Wright were after the System—not
merely its pieces.

A major source of the power of *Native Son* derived from Wright's
ability to articulate the relevant rituals of black and white cultures
—and Bigger's response to them. These rituals emphasize the presence in culture of rational drive, curiosity, revolutionary will, individualism, self-consciousness (preoccupations of Western culture)
—or their absence.

Thus blindness (shared by white and black cultures), softness,
shrinking from life, escapism, otherworldliness, abjectness, and surrender are the meaning of the black cultural rituals from which
Bigger recoils, and the counters with which blacks are allowed to
purchase their meager allowance of shelter and bread. They contrast sharply with Bigger's (the outsider's) deep urges for freedom
of gesture and spontaneous response to existence. Wright's indict-

[1] Richard Wright, *Native Son* (New York: Signet, 1961), pp. 23–24.
[2] *Ibid.*, p. 62.
[3] Webb, p. 205. [Constance Webb, *Richard Wright, A Biography* (New York:
G. P. Putnam's Sons, 1968)—Ed.]

ment is that these negative qualities are systematically programmed into black culture by the all-powerful white oppressor.

Having murdered the white girl Mary Dalton—thus defying the imprisoning white oppressor, Bigger Thomas feels a rush of energy that makes him equal to the oppressor. He now explains his revolt against black culture. Buddy, his brother, is "soft and vague; his eyes were defenseless and their glance went only to the surface of things." Buddy is "aimless, lost, with no sharp or hard edges, like a chubby puppy." There is in him "a certain stillness, an isolation, meaninglessness." [4]

Bigger's sister Vera, "seemed to be shrinking from life with every gesture she made." His mother has religion in place of whiskey, and his girlfriend Bessie has whiskey in place of religion. In the last section of *Native Son*, his mother's epiphany is her crawling on her knees from one white Dalton to the other to beg for the life of Bigger. In "Flight," the second part of the novel, Bessie's epiphany is a prose blues complaint concerning the trap of her life, and then in a terrible sigh that surrenders to Bigger her entire will, she betrays her life completely. Finally, after Bigger is captured, a black minister epiphanizes the version of religious passivity that insured endurance of aimless and cramped life, as he unsuccessfully appeals to the captured Bigger. The gestures and rituals of the black minister are rendered with masterly brilliance.

In contrast, the symbols, rituals, and personalities of the white culture express directness, spontaneous freedom, at-homeness in the universe, will—and tyranny. While Bigger concentrates upon avoiding answering questions from the Communist Jan Erlone and the liberal Mary Dalton in yes or no terms, he is confounded by their ability to act and speak simply and directly. In a very fine scene that evidences Wright's great novelistic talent, their very freedom and liberality dramatize his oppression and shame. Their gestures say that it is their universe. And the fact that Jan Erlone and Mary Dalton, in seconds, can, as individuals, suspend all racial restraints underlines the habitual racial rigidities ingrained in Bigger's life, which deprive him of spontaneous gesture. Oppressively, "To Bigger and his kind white people were not really people; they were a sort of great natural force, like a stormy sky looming overhead, or like a deep swirling river stretching suddenly at one's feet in the dark." The white world is the "white blur," "white walls," "the snow,"—

[4] *Native Son*, p. 103.

all of which place Bigger in the condition of the desperate rat with which *Native Son* begins.

The Jan Erlone–Dalton group of whites express the rituals meditated by a sufficient humanism to partially obscure their relationship to a brutal system. They inspire Bigger's hatred but also a measure of bewilderment. Even the elder Dalton can be nice because the System does the work. With one hand he functions in a company that restricts blacks to ghettos and squeezes from them high rents for rat-infested, cramped apartments; with the other, and without conscious irony, he gives substantial sums to black uplift organizations. Although the Dalton's kindness cannot extend to sparing Bigger's life (since he has murdered their daughter—the flower of the system), he will prevent the ejection of Bigger's family from its rat-dominated apartment.

The liberalism of the Communist Jan Erlone, his girl friend sympathizer Mary Dalton, and the rest of the Dalton family function as esthetic rituals that create an easy-going atmosphere for sullen submission and inhibition. In the militarized zone are the racial rituals of Detective Britten bouncing Bigger's head against the wall and spitting out definitions of blacks that deny their life. Then there are the agents of the mass media, the rhetoricians, the police, and the mob.

Bigger standing equally outside the shrinking black culture and the hard-driving white culture can only feel the existential choice demanded by his compulsion toward the heritage of man shoving upward from his guts, and sense that something very terrible must happen to him. Near the end he is tortured by the knowledge that his deepest hunger is for human communion, and by his lawyer's briefly raising it as a possibility. But the mirage is soon exposed and he must warm himself by the bleak embers of his hard-won and lonely existential knowledge: ". . . what I killed for, I am!"

It is part of the greatness of *Native Son* that it survives a plethora of flaws. For example, despite Wright's indictment of white society, he shows in his major fiction little knowledge that, while black life is stifled by brutality, the private realities of white life find it increasingly impossible to free themselves from the imprisoning blandishments of a neurotic culture. His failure to image this fact, although we have seen that he had some understanding of it, makes it seem that Bigger's problems would have been solved by his entry into the white world. The great engagement of the universe that rages through the first and second parts of the novel sputters, at points, in the third part while Wright scores debater's points on jobs, housing, and equal opportunity. The famous courtroom speech that the attorney Max makes in behalf of Bigger hardly rises above such humanitarian matters. Thus a novel that resounds in revolutionary tones descends to merely reformist modulations that would make glad the heart of a New Deal liberal.

As the theme and situations of the novel increase in density of implication, Wright is too frequently touching the reader's elbow to explain reactions and make distinctions that are too complex for Bigger to verbalize. The style, therefore, fails at crucial points. Melodrama, as in the murder of Mary Dalton, is sometimes very functional. At other times, it is unfortunately its own excuse for being.

And so one may go on, but when he finishes he will find *Native Son* still afloat and waiting for the next reader to make it a reference point in the fabric of his being.

Wright's vision of black men and women rendered in the four books that I have discussed [5] stormed its way into the fabric of American culture with such fury that its threads form a reference point in the thinking and imagination of those who have yet to read him. Quickly downgraded as more art-conscious black writers made the scene, he seems now all too prophetic, and all too relevant, majestically waiting that close critical engagement which forms the greatest respect that can be paid to a great man and writer.

Thus, today, when we think that we know so much about black life, even down to its metaphysics and ambiguity, it is humbling to realize that the lifelong commitment of soul that was Richard Wright is of the essence of much that we think we know.

---

[5] [The four works are *Black Boy, Uncle Tom's Children, Native Son,* and *Lawd Today.*—Ed.]

Wright's Invisible Native Son

by Donald B. Gibson

The difficulty most critics have who write about Richard Wright's *Native Son* is that they do not see Bigger Thomas.[1] They see him with their outer eyes, but not with the inner eyes, "those eyes with which they look through their physical eyes upon reality."[2] Of course there is a certain sense in which everyone is invisible, a certain sense in which the observer creates the observed, attributing to him qualities whose nature depends upon the viewer's own character. When we see a man in muddy work clothes, we are likely to see him only as a laborer and to have aroused in us whatever ideas we have toward laborers. We rarely look at a man so dressed (assuming that he is unknown to us) and see a father, a churchgoer, taxpayer or fisherman, though the man underneath the clothing may theoretically be all these things. If we think about him, we automatically assume certain things about his life style—about his values, his economic and social position, and even his occupation. To the extent that the clothes determine what we see, the person beneath them is invisible to us.

"Wright's Invisible Native Son" by Donald B. Gibson. From American Quar-terly, *XXI, No. 4 (1969), 728–38. Copyright © 1969 by the University of Pennsylvania. Published with the permission of the author, the Trustees of the University of Pennsylvania, and* American Quarterly.

[1] Limitations of space preclude naming all the critics I have in mind. A few of them are the following: James Baldwin, "Everybody's Protest Novel" and "Many Thousands Gone," *Notes of a Native Son* (Boston, 1955), pp. 13–23, 24–45; Robert Bone, *The Negro Novel in America* (New Haven, 1958), pp. 140–52; Hugh M. Gloster, *Negro Voices in American Fiction* (Chapel Hill, N.C., 1948), pp. 222–34; John Reilly, "Afterword," *Native Son* (New York, 1966). Critics most nearly exceptions are: Edwin Berry Burgum, *The Novel and the World's Dilemma* (New York, 1963), pp. 223–40; Esther Merle Jackson, "The American Negro and the Image of the Absurd," *Phylon*, XXIII (1962), 359–71; Nathan A. Scott, "Search for Beliefs: The Fiction of Richard Wright," *University of Kansas City Review*, XXIII (1956), 19–24.

[2] Ralph Ellison, *Invisible Man* (New York, 1952), p. 3.

The difficulty comes about when we assume that the outer covering is the essential person. Most critics of Wright's novel see only the outer covering of Bigger Thomas, the blackness of his skin and his resulting social role. Few have seen him as a discrete entity, a particular person who struggles with the burden of his humanity. Wright has gone to great lengths in the novel to create Bigger as a person, to invest the social character with particularizing traits, to delineate the features of a face. The final meaning of the book, as a matter of fact, depends upon the awareness on the part of the reader of Bigger's individuality. The lack of such awareness has led most critics to misread the novel, for almost all of them interpret it as though the social person, Bigger Thomas, were the *real* and *essential* person. The following bit of dialogue, however, suggests a different perspective.

> Max: "Well, this thing's bigger than you, son. . . ."
> Bigger: "They going to kill me anyhow." [3]

This exchange between Max and Bigger reveals that each is looking at the problem at hand in an essentially different way. Max is thinking of the social implications of the situation; Bigger's attention is focused on his own impending doom. Which view is the truer, the more significant in the context of the novel? Wright's critics have generally opted for the view of Max, but if Max's view is true, then most of the whole final section does not make sense. For a careful reading of that third section, "Fate," indicates that the focus of the novel is not on the trial nor on Max, but on Bigger and on his finally successful attempt to come to terms with his imminent death. It need be noted that the trial does not take up the entire third section of the novel as has been often said. In the edition cited above, the third section comprises 126 pages; the trial itself consumes 37 pages and Max's address to the jury, 17 pages. The length of Max's speech and its bearing on what has preceded in the novel to that point have led experienced readers to neglect what else happens in that final section. It has led to many conclusions about the novel which are not borne out by the 89 pages of the last section describing what happens before and after the trial. The degree to which the reader focuses upon Max and Max's speech determines the degree to which Bigger is invisible to him.

In order to assess properly the meaning of the final section, it is

[3] *Native Son* (New York, 1940), p. 312. Subsequent quotations from the novel are from this edition.

necessary to understand what happens in the concluding pages of the novel. First of all it is too simple to say as Baldwin does that "he [Bigger] *wants* to die because he glories in his hatred and prefers, like Lucifer, rather to rule in hell than serve in heaven." [4] The point is that Bigger, through introspection, finally arrives at a definition of self which is his own and different from that assigned to him by everyone else in the novel. The many instances in the last of the three sections of the novel which show him exploring his deepest thoughts, feelings and emotions reveal Baldwin's statement to be patently false. Shortly after Bigger's capture and imprisonment he lies thinking in his cell.

> And, under and above it all, there was the fear of death before which he was naked and without defense; he had to go forward and meet his end like any other living thing upon the earth. . . . There would have to hover above him, like the stars in a full sky, a vast configuration of images and symbols whose magic and power could lift him up and make him live so intensely that the dread of being black and unequal would be forgotten; that even death would not matter, that it would be a victory. This would have to happen before he could look them in the face again: a new pride and a new humility would have to be born in him, a humility springing from a new identification with some part of the world in which he lived, and this identification forming the basis for a new hope that would function in him as pride and dignity. (pp. 234–35)

This quotation not only refutes Baldwin's statement about Bigger's motivations, but it as well indicates the focus of the novel at this point is on Bigger Thomas the private person. The emphasis is upon a problem that he faces as an isolated, solitary human whose problem is compounded by race though absolutely not defined by racial considerations. There follows from the point in the novel during which the above quotation occurs a pattern of advance and retrogression as Bigger gropes his way, privately and alone, toward that "new identification," that "pride and dignity" referred to in the passage. From this point on Bigger feels by turns guilt, hate, shame, remorse, fear, anger, and through the knowledge of himself engendered through acquaintance with his basic thoughts and feelings moves toward a sense of identity. There is a good deal of emphasis placed upon the solitary nature of his problem. At least twice he advances to the point at which he recognizes that salvation for

[4] *Notes of a Native Son*, p. 44.

him can come only from himself, from his own effort and knowledge.

> He was balanced on a hair-line now, but there was no one to push him forward or backward, no one to make him feel that he had any value or worth—no one but himself. (p. 305)

> He believed that Max knew how he felt, and once more before he died he wanted to talk with him and feel with as much keenness as possible what his living and dying meant. That was all the hope he had now. If there were any sure and firm knowledge for him, it would have to come from himself. (p. 350)

If we see the quotation above (from pp. 233–35) as defining Bigger's essential problem, then it is evident that the passage must have relevance to the concluding pages of the novel. When Bigger has achieved the "new humility," the "pride and dignity" referred to there, if he has achieved it, it should be evidenced somewhere later in the novel. And so it is. During the final two pages of the novel it is clear that Bigger no longer suffers, is no longer in terror about his impending death. "Aw, I reckon I believe in myself. . . . I ain't got nothing else. . . . I got to die" (p. 358—Wright's ellipses). He accepts himself as never before, and in realizing his identity is able to evaluate his past actions objectively. "I didn't want to kill! . . . But what I killed for, I *am*! It must have been pretty deep in me to make me kill! I must have felt it awful hard to murder. . . ."

Because he has come to terms with himself, because he no longer hates and despises himself as he has during most of his life, it is no longer necessary for him to feel hatred. For this reason he is able to pass along through Max a reassuring word to his mother: "Just go and tell Ma I was all right and not to worry none, see? Tell her I was all right and wasn't crying none . . ." (p. 358). Had he "died in hatred," as Bone says,[5] he would hardly have called out his final words to Max, "Tell Jan hello . . ." (p. 359). These words indicate that Bigger's contradictory feelings about himself and his situation have been resolved, for they could only be spoken by virtue of Bigger's having accepted the consequences of his actions and hence himself. He has no choice—if he is to achieve the degree of reconciliation to his fate necessary for him to face death and therefore assert his humanity—but to recognize that he *is* what he has *done*.

The two perspectives of Bigger Thomas contained in the novel

---

[5] *The Negro Novel*, p. 150.

exist in tension until in the final pages the focus shifts away entirely from the social emphasis. No matter what the social implications of Bigger's situation, the fact is that he, the private, isolated human must face the consequences. It is no wonder that Bigger is almost totally unable to understand Max's speech during the trial. He grasps something of the tone, but the meanings of the words escape him, for Max is not really thinking about Bigger the existential person, the discrete human entity. When Bigger and Max converse privately, they understand each other reasonably well. But during the trial Max is talking about a symbol, a representative figure. Hence the significant problem becomes not whether Max will save Bigger—the answer to that question is a foregone conclusion—but whether Bigger will save himself in the only possible way, by coming to terms with himself. This we see him doing as we observe him during long, solitary hours of minute introspection and self-analysis.

Probably the critic most responsible for the perception of Bigger Thomas as a social entity and that alone is James Baldwin, who conceived some rather convincing arguments about the limitations of the protest novel and especially of *Native Son*.

> All of Bigger's life is controlled, defined by his hatred and his fear. And later, his fear drives him to murder and his hatred to rape; he dies, having come, through this violence, we are told, for the first time, to a kind of life, having for the first time redeemed his manhood.[6]

Baldwin, for all the persuasiveness of his language, has failed to see Bigger the person. For it is clear enough that Bigger's feeling of elation, of having done a creative thing simply in murdering is not the final outcome. It is rather early in the novel when he feels release, free from the forces which have all his life constrained him. But after his capture he finds he is indeed not free; he still has himself to cope with. His final feeling is not—as the concluding pages of the novel explicitly show—exaltation for having "redeemed his manhood." Very soon after the first murder, to be sure, he does feel that it has had some redeeming effect.

> The thought of what he had done, the awful horror of it, the daring associated with such actions, formed for him for the first time in his fear-ridden life a barrier of protection between him and a world he feared. He had murdered and had created a new

⁶ *Notes of a Native Son*, p. 22.

life for himself. It was something that was all his own, and it was the first time in his life he had had anything that others could not take from him. (p. 90)

But this response occurs after all about one-fourth of the way through the novel. These are not the feelings Bigger has at the end. One need only imagine this passage as among Bigger's thoughts as we last see him in order to see how inappropriate it would be as a concluding statement. He is not in the mood of prideful self-assertion which he feels so often from the time he disposes of Mary's body until his crime is discovered. Instead, the conclusion finds him feeling a calm assurance and acceptance of self. There is neither irony nor condescension in his final "Tell Jan hello," nor does the last scene in the denotative meanings of its words and the tone project "hatred and fear" on Bigger's part.

Baldwin's eloquent statement at the end of "Everybody's Protest Novel," describing how the protest novel fails does not describe the content of Wright's novel.

> The failure of the protest novel lies in its rejection of life, the human being, the denial of his beauty, dread, power, in its insistence that it is his categorization alone which is real and which cannot be transcended.[7]

The statement itself is not to be questioned; its applicability to *Native Son* is. There is too much in Wright's novel which suggests that Bigger's response to his situation does not stem from his categorization, his Negroness, but from his humanness. What has the following response, occurring after Bigger has returned from hearing his sentence, to do with his "categorization"?

> In self-defense he shut out the night and day from his mind, for if he had thought of the sun's rising and setting, of the moon or the stars, of clouds or rain, he would have died a thousand deaths before they took him to the chair. To accustom his mind to death as much as possible, he made all the world beyond his cell a vast grey land where neither night nor day was, peopled by strange men and women whom he could not understand, but with those lives he longed to mingle once before he went. (p. 349)

These are not the thoughts and feelings of a Negro, as such, but of

---

[7] P. 23. Edward Margolies explores the opposite view of Wright's novel in *Native Sons: A Critical Study of Twentieth-Century American Authors* (New York, 1968), pp. 85–86.

a man who is about to die and who struggles to cope with the fact. Race, social condition, whatever category a reader might have placed him in, have no relevance here. There are many such passages in the third section of the book showing Bigger's individual response to his situation. For example, the following:

> He had lived and acted on the assumption that he was alone, and now he saw that he had not been. What he had done made others suffer. No matter how much he would long for them to forget him, they would not be able to. His family was a part of him, not only in blood, but in spirit. (p. 254)
>
> He would not mind dying now if he could only find out what this meant, what he was in relation to all the others that lived, and the earth upon which he stood. Was there some battle everybody was fighting, and he had missed it? (p. 307)
>
> His face rested against the bars and he felt tears roll down his cheeks. His wet lips tasted salt. He sank to his knees and sobbed: "I don't want to die. . . . I don't want to die. . . ." (p. 308)

His interpretation of the opening scene of the novel is likewise a measure of the degree to which Baldwin does not see Bigger.

> Rats live there too in the Thomas apartment . . . and we first encounter Bigger in the act of killing one. One may consider that the entire book, from that harsh "Brring!" to Bigger's weak "Goodby" as the lawyer, Max, leaves him in the death cell is an extension, with the roles inverted, of this chilling metaphor.[8]

This interpretation would be true if Bigger were *only* the social figure which critics have seen. But the figure on the final pages of the novel, no matter what he is, is not a rat. He does not die as a rat dies; he is neither fearful nor desperate.

An alternative reading is offered by Edwin Burgum in his essay on *Native Son* in which he says of Bigger's killing of the rat and flaunting it in the faces of his mother and sister, "His courage is that overcompensation for fear called bravado. It passes beyond the needs of the situation and defeats its own end here as in later crises in the novel." [9] This interpretation gets beyond the problem of comparing Bigger with a rat. Certainly Wright's sympathies are with Bigger to a greater degree than his being likened to a rat implies.

[8] [*Notes of a Native Son*] p. 34.
[9] [*The Novel and the World's Dilemma*] p. 232.

It must be admitted that Bigger Thomas, the social figure whom Baldwin and others have seen, has a prominent place in the novel and is by no means a figment. He is a representative figure to Buckley, to the policemen investigating the murder of Mary, and to the public at large. Wright makes it amply evident that the desire on the part of these people to do away with Bigger reflects a primitive desire to perform ritual murder and, thereby, to do away with the potential threat posed by all other Negroes through sacrificing the representative black figure. But readers need to avoid the error of the characters in the novel by distinguishing between Bigger's qualities as a representative figure and his qualities as a particular person (difficult though this may be in our time and in our society) who, exclusive of race, faces death.

> If he were nothing, if this were all, then why could not he die without hesitancy? Who and what was he to feel the agony of a wonder so intensely that it amounted to fear? Why was this strange impulse always throbbing in him when there was nothing outside of him to meet it and explain it? Who or what had traced this restless design in him? Why was this eternal reaching for something that was not there? Why this black gulf between him and the world: warm red blood here and cold blue sky there, and never a wholeness, a oneness, a meeting of the two? (pp. 350–51)

Feeling such things as these and about to die in the electric chair, Bigger ceases to be representative of the Negro and becomes every man whose death is imminent—that is, every man.

The view of Bigger as representative (and hence invisible) comes about in part because Wright's novel has been too frequently seen as a "Negro" novel or a protest novel, and all the limitations of these categories have been ascribed to it. It has been extremely difficult for even the most sophisticated readers to see Bigger's humanity because the idea of an ignorant, uneducated, criminal Negro coming to terms with the human condition, as Bigger finally does, is an alien idea. The novel should be compared not only to *Crime and Punishment*, the work with which it is most frequently compared, but with *The Stranger* as well. Wright's and Camus' novels were published two years apart (1940 and 1942 respectively), and there are many striking parallels between them. The most fruitful result of such a comparison may be to lift Wright's novel out of the context of the racial problem in America and to place it in larger perspective, or at least to reveal the extent to which *Native Son* is not so limited as it has appeared to be.

The limited view has also been responsible for the interpretation of the novel as a propaganda piece for the Communist Party.[10] On the contrary the novel points up the limitations of a system of ideas which by its very nature is incapable of dealing with certain basic human problems. Bigger is saved in the end, but not through the efforts of the Party, which constantly asserts that the individual cannot achieve meaningful salvation. This further implies that the thought processes leading to Wright's break with the Party were already in motion as early as 1939, and that his formal public announcement of the break in 1944 [11] was a resolution of much earlier distress.

The interpretation of the novel as a propaganda piece for the Communist Party stems from the notion that Max is Wright's spokesman. As a result, a good deal of weight is placed upon Max's address to the jury. Though there is enough evidence to suggest that Max's personal view of Bigger allows for his existence as a discrete individual, the strategy he chooses to defend Bigger requires that he deal with him largely on an abstract level with the intention of convincing his hearers that the abstraction is embodied within the particular individual before them. Thus he says:

> "This boy represents but a tiny aspect of a problem whose reality sprawls over a third of this nation." (p. 330)
> "Multiply Bigger Thomas twelve million times, allowing for environmental and temperamental variations, and for those Negroes who are completely under the influence of the church, and you have the psychology of the Negro people." (p. 333)

The effect of his words on many is simply to enhance Bigger's invisibility.

Rather than being Wright's spokesman, in truth, Max presents one side of a dialogue whose totality is expressed through the dual perspective contained in the novel.[12] Max is indeed a sympathetic character, but for all his good intentions, he has limitations. He never, for example, entirely understands what Bigger is getting at during their conversations. Only in the end, during their final meeting, does he come to have some notion of the fact that he is not

---

[10] Richard Sullivan, "Afterword" to *Native Son*, Signet, 1961.

[11] "I Tried to Be a Communist," *Atlantic Monthly*, CLXV (Aug. 1944), 61–70; (Sept. 1944), 48–56.

[12] Margolies believes that the duality of perspective referred to here is unresolved. Pp. 79–80.

superior to Bigger, that he knows no more than Bigger about the kinds of questions the condemned man is asking and consequently is not in a position to explain anything. When Bigger tells Max that he *is* what he has *done* ("What I killed for, I *am!*), Max's response is to recoil in horror, for even he ultimately is unable to accept any definition of man outside his own preconceived idea. Max cannot accept the implications of Bigger's conclusions nor, indeed, can he fully understand the position that Bigger has finally arrived at. Wright makes this point doubly clear with the line, "Max groped for his hat like a blind man." Now given the nearly explicit meanings which sight and blindness have had in the novel prior to this, it can hardly be a fortuitous simile. Not even Max is completely capable of recognizing and accepting the truth of Bigger's humanity.

Though Max's motivations are good, founded as they are upon his basic good character and good feeling, he is unable finally to save Bigger, for Bigger's salvation comes about through his own efforts, through his eventual ability to find freedom from the constraints of his past. All the characters in Wright's major works after *Native Son* achieve the same kind of freedom, or at least the promise of such freedom, in one way or another. This is true of the central character of *Black Boy* (which is more fictional in technique and intention than commonly recognized), *The Long Dream, The Outsider* and of "The Man Who Lived Underground." *Native Son* resolves the tension between the two alternatives, the one seeing the salvation of individuals through social change, the other seeing the salvation of individuals through their own efforts. After *Native Son* Wright was never again to suggest the possibility of any individual's achieving meaningful social salvation. The inescapable conclusion is that Wright lost faith entirely in social solutions to human problems and came to believe that ultimately the individual alone can save himself. During that final meeting between Max and Bigger it is made abundantly clear that Bigger has through the course of the third section of the novel come to terms with his most pressing problem, his impending doom. In so doing he achieves the only meaningful salvation possible. (Max speaks first.)

> "But on both sides men want to live; men are fighting for life. Who will win? Well, the side . . . with the most humanity and the most men. That's why . . . y-you've got to b-believe in yourself, Bigger. . . ."

Max's head jerked up in surprise when Bigger laughed.
"Aw, I reckon I believe in myself. . . . I ain't got nothing else.
. . . I got to die." (p. 358)

Now if the conclusions I have come to here are valid, then two
highly significant corollaries follow: (1) Wright did not *simply*
emerge from the naturalistic school of Dreiser, Dos Passos and Farrell; he did not simply adapt the techniques and thoughts of the
naturalists to the situation of the black man.[13] (2) The existentialist
thinking of his later work did not derive from the influence on him
of Camus, Sartre and other French existentialists, but grew out of
his own experience in America.[14]

I do not want to argue that Wright was not strongly influenced
by American literary naturalism; certainly he was. But he was not
as confined by the tradition as has been generally believed. If my
thesis about *Native Son* is correct, then Wright is not an author
whose major novel reflects the final phases of a dying tradition, but
he is instead one who out of the thought, techniques and general
orientation of the naturalistic writers developed beyond their scope.
Native Son, as I have described it in this essay, looks forward rather
than backward. It is a prototype of the modern existentialist novel
and a link between the fiction of the 1930s and a good deal of more
modern fiction.

A kind of condescension and a preconception about the potential
of a self-educated black man from the very depths of the South have
combined to obscure the sources of Wright's proclivity toward existentialism. The following comments made by two writers and critics who were friends of Wright make the point.

REDDING: Dick was a small-town boy—a small-town Missis-
                sippi boy—all of his days. The hog maw and the
                collard greens. He was fascinated by the existential-
                ist group for a while, but he didn't really under-
                stand them.

BONTEMPS: Essentially, of course, Wright was and remained not
                only an American but a Southerner. Negroes have
                a special fondness for that old saw, "You can take
                the boy out of the country, but you can't take the
                country out of the boy." [15]

[13] Wright's relation to the naturalistic tradition was first articulated by Alfred
Kazin, *On Native Grounds* (New York, 1942), p. 372, and later by Bone in
The Negro Novel, pp. 142–43.
[14] Margolies concurs with this conclusion. P. 68.
[15] Saunders Redding and Arna Bontemps in "Reflections on Richard Wright:

In order to understand the sources of the existentialist concern in Wright's work and thought, one need only note the quality and character of the life described by Wright in *Black Boy* and realize as well that "existentialism" may be described as a mood arising out of the exigencies of certain life situations rather than as a fully developed and articulated systematic philosophy which one chooses to hold or rejects. Though we cannot say that existentialism resulted directly from the experience of Europeans under Nazi occupation, we can certainly say that the occupation, the war itself, created circumstances conducive to the nurturing and development of the existential response. Europeans during the war, especially those engaged in underground activities, daily faced the imminent possibility of death, and the constant awareness of impending death was largely responsible for the emergence of a way of interpreting the meaning of life consonant with that awareness. *Black Boy* of course does not describe a wartime situation, but one cannot help but feel the constant pressure on the person described there, a pressure from a world which threatens unceasingly to destroy him. The earliest of Wright's memories is of an episode which results in his being beaten unconscious, and this at a very young age. Thereafter we see described in the book the progress of an inward, alienated individual, distrustful of all external authority, who learns that his survival depends upon the repudiation of the values of others and a strong reliance upon his own private and personal sense of values. The existential precept, "existence precedes essence," stems as a mood from Wright's experience as decribed in *Black Boy,* but as a condition of his life and not as a consciously held philosophical principle. Herein lie the sources of Bigger Thomas' response to the condition brought about by his crime, capture and condemnation.

A comment made by Wright in response to an unfriendly review of *Native Son* is relevant as a final observation.

> If there had been one person in the Dalton household who viewed Bigger Thomas as a human being, the crime would have been solved in half an hour. Did not Bigger himself know that it was the denial of his personality that enabled him to escape detection so long? The one piece of incriminating evidence which would

---

A Symposium," *Anger and Beyond,* ed., Herbert Hill (New York, 1966), p. 207. Further comments on Wright and existentialism occur on pages 203, 205, 208, 209.

have solved the "murder mystery" was Bigger's humanity under
their very eyes.[16]

We need only make the proper substitutions to see the relevance of
Wright's comment to the views of most critics of his novel. "The
denial of his personality," and the failure on their part to see "Bigger's humanity under their very eyes" have caused him to be invisible, to be Wright's own invisible native son.

[16] "I Bite the Hand that Feeds Me," *Atlantic Monthly,* CLXV (June 1940),
826.

Introduction to the First Edition

by Dorothy Canfield Fisher

How to produce neuroses in sheep and psychopathic upsets in rats and other animals has been known to research psychologists for so long that accounts of these experiments have filtered out to us, the general public, through books and periodicals. The process seems to be a simple one: the animal is trained to react in certain ways to certain stimuli, and then is placed in a situation in which these reactions are impossible. After making a number of attempts to go on reacting as he has been trained to, each attempt blocked, the frustration produces a nervous breakdown. His actions become abnormal, quite different from what is natural to him in health. The sheep, by definition gregarious, becomes solitary and morose, he will neither mingle with his fellows nor eat nor drink as he usually does, nor react in a normal manner to any stimuli, even the simplest and most familiar. The rat continues madly to dash his head against the locked door until, bruised and bleeding, he has battered himself to exhaustion, almost to death.

The National Youth Commission, of which Mr. Owen D. Young is Chairman, includes, among its projects for research into the condition of American youth, an investigation as to what is offered Negro Youth by the U.S.A. The first statement made in a report recently sent in to the Commission by the specialists assigned to this field, reads:

"The four area research studies just completed by the staff of the American Youth Commission concerned with an analysis of the minority status of Negro youth present conclusive evidence that large percentages of Negro youth by virtue of their combined handicap of racial barriers and low social position subtly reflect in their own personality-traits minor or major distortions or deficiencies which

---

compound their problem of personality adjustment in American society. More specifically, the research studies have revealed: That being a Negro in most cases not only means living in the presence of severe physical limitations, but, more important for personality development, also means living in an intimate culture *whose incentives, rewards, and punishments prevent the development of that type of personal standards, attitudes, and habits which the general community deems desirable.*"

In other words, our American society creates around all youth (as every society does) a continual pressure of suggestion to try to live up to the accepted ideals of the country—such ordinary, traditional, taken-for-granted American ideals as to fight injustice fearlessly; to cringe to no man; to choose one's own life work; to resist with stout-hearted self-respect affronts to decent human dignity, whether one's own or others'; to drive ahead toward honestly earned success, all sails spread to the old American wind blowing from the Declaration of Independence. But our society puts Negro youth in the situation of the animal in the psychological laboratory in which a neurosis is to be caused, by making it impossible for him to try to live up to those never-to-be-questioned national ideals, as other young Americans do.

Native Son is the first report in fiction we have had from those who succumb to these distracting cross-currents of contradictory nerve-impulses, from those whose behavior-patterns give evidence of the same bewildered, senseless tangle of abnormal nerve-reactions studied in animals by psychologists in laboratory experiments.

It is not surprising that this novel plumbs blacker depths of human experience than American literature has yet had, comparable only to Dostoievski's revelation of human misery in wrong-doing.

I do not at all mean to imply that *Native Son* as literature is comparable to the masterpieces of Dostoievski (although I think there is no one single effect in Dostoievski finer than the last page of *Native Son* in which—just before he dies, not having yet lived—the stultified Negro boy is born at last into humanity and makes his first simple, normal human response to a fellow-man). What I mean to say is only that the author of this book, as has no other American writer, wrestles with utter sincerity with the Dostoievski subject—a human soul in hell because it is sick with a deadly spiritual sickness.

This is really all I have to say about this absorbing story of a "bad Negro," except to warn away from it, urgently, those who do not like to read books which harrow them up. It can be guaranteed to harrow up any human heart capable of compassion or honest self-questioning.

Yet, perhaps, it would be well to add two more short comments. One is to remind the reader that Bigger's mother and sister, although subjected to exactly the same psychological cross-currents as he, are not bad but good—the hymn-singing, submissive, all-enduring, religious, affront-swallowing yes-massa-ing Negroes, so heartily approved by white people looking for cheap help "to do their work for them." They are, as much as Bigger, in accordance with the experiments in psychological laboratories. For not all sheep fall into bewildered nervous breakdowns, not all rats become psychotic. Some —are they the ones which are placid? or insensitive?—simply take what comes to them, without losing their normal appetite for living. There is no sounder stroke of realism in *Native Son* than the portrait of Bigger's sweet-natured, infinitely patient, unrebelling doormat of a mother.

The other point I would like to make is that the author shows genuine literary skill in the construction of his novel in giving so few pages to show us in concrete detail the exact ways in which American society constantly stimulates the powerful full-blooded human organism to action, which is as constantly forbidden to him by our mores.

Mr. Wright does not prove to us, in one realistic incident after another, taken from the childhood and youth of his hero, that the outlets to native power which would have been open to any white boy were closed to Bigger. He knows he does not need to prove this. With a bold stroke of literary divination, he assumes that every one of his American readers will know all that without being told. And he is right. We do.

Richard Wright: The Case
of Bigger Thomas

by Malcolm Cowley

Native Son is the most impressive American novel I have read
since *The Grapes of Wrath*. In some ways the two books resemble
each other: both deal with the dispossessed and both grew out of the
radical movement of the 1930's. There is, however, a distinction to
be drawn between the motives of the two authors. Steinbeck, more
privileged than the characters in his novel, wrote out of deep pity
for them, and the fault he had to avoid was sentimentality. Richard
Wright, a Negro, was moved by wrongs he had suffered in his own
person, and what he had to fear was a blind anger that might destroy the pity in him, making him hate any character whose skin
was whiter than his own. His first book, *Uncle Tom's Children*, had
not completely avoided that fault. It was a collection of stories all
but one of which had the same pattern: a Negro was goaded into
killing one or more white men and was killed in turn, without feeling regret for himself or his victims. Some of the stories I found
physically painful to read, even though I admired them. So deep
was the author's sense of the indignities heaped on his race that one
felt he was revenging himself by a whole series of symbolic murders.
In *Native Son* the pattern is the same, but the author's sympathies
have broadened and his resentment, though quite as deep, is less
painful and personal.

The hero, Bigger Thomas, is a Negro boy of twenty, a poolroom
loafer, a bully, a liar and a petty thief. "Bigger, sometimes I wonder
why I birthed you," his pious mother tells him. "Honest, you the
most no-countest man I ever seen in all my life." A Chicago philanthropist tries to help the family by hiring him as chauffeur. That

"*Richard Wright: The Case of Bigger Thomas*" from Think Back on Us . . .
A Contemporary Chronicle of the 1930s *by Malcolm Cowley. Edited with an
Introduction by Henry Dan Piper. Copyright © 1967 by Southern Illinois Uni-
versity Press. Reprinted by permission of Southern Illinois University Press.*

same night Bigger kills the philanthropist's daughter—out of fear of being discovered in her room—and stuffs her body into the furnace. This half-accidental crime leads to others. Bigger tries to cast the blame for the girl's disappearance on her lover, a Communist; he tries to collect a ransom from her parents; after the body is found he murders his Negro mistress to keep her from betraying him to the police. The next day he is captured on the snow-covered roof of a South Side tenement, while a mob howls in the street below.

In the last part of the book, which is also the best, we learn that the case of Bigger Thomas is not the author's deepest concern. Behind it is another, more complicated story he is trying hard to explain, though the words come painfully at first, and later come in a flood that almost sweeps him away. "Listen, you white folks," he seems to be saying over and over. "I want to tell you about all the Negroes in America. I want to tell you how they live and how they feel. I want you to change your minds about them before it is too late to prevent a worse disaster than any we have known. I speak for my own people, but I speak for America too." And because he does speak for and to the nation, without ceasing to be a Negro, his book has more force than any other American novel by a member of his race.

Bigger, he explains, had been trained from the beginning to be a bad citizen. He had been taught American ideals of life, in the schools, in the magazines, in the cheap movie houses, but had been denied any means of achieving them. Everything he wanted to have or do was reserved for the whites. "I just can't get used to it," he tells one of his poolroom buddies. "I swear to God I can't. . . . Every time I think about it I feel like somebody's poking a red-hot iron down my throat."

At the trial, his white-haired Jewish lawyer makes a final plea to the judge for mercy. "What Bigger Thomas did early that Sunday morning in the Dalton home and what he did that Sunday night in the empty building was but a tiny aspect of what he had been doing all his life long. He was *living*, only as he knew how, and as we have forced him to live. . . . The hate and fear which we have inspired in him, woven by our civilization into the very structure of his consciousness, into his blood and bones, into the hourly functioning of his personality, have become the justification of his existence. . . . Every thought he thinks is potential murder."

This long courtroom speech, which sums up the argument of the novel, is at once its strongest and its weakest point. It is strongest when Mr. Max is making a plea for the American Negroes in general. "They are not simply twelve million people; in reality they constitute a separate nation, stunted, stripped and held captive *within* this nation." Many of them—and many white people too— are full of "balked longing for some kind of fulfillment and exultation"; and their existence is "what makes our future seem a looming image of violence." In this context, Mr. Max's talk of another civil war seems not so much a threat as an agonized warning. But his speech is weakest as a plea for the individual life of Bigger Thomas. It did not convince the judge, and I doubt that it will convince many readers.

It is not that I think Bigger "deserved" the death sentence for his two murders. Most certainly his guilt was shared by the society that condemned him. But when he killed Mary Dalton he was performing the first free action in his whole fear-tortured life; he was accepting his first moral responsibility. That is what he tried so hard to explain to his lawyer. "I ain't worried none about them women I killed. . . . I killed 'em 'cause I was scared and mad. But I been scared and mad all my life and after I killed that first woman, I wasn't scared no more for a little while." And when his lawyer asks him if he ever thought he would face the electric chair, "Now I come to think of it," he answers, "it seems like something like this just had to be." If Mr. Max had managed to win a life sentence for Bigger Thomas, he would have robbed him of his only claim to human courage and dignity. But that Richard Wright makes us feel this, while setting out to prove something else—that he makes Bigger Thomas a human rather than a racial symbol—shows that he wrote an even better novel than he had planned.

Remembering Richard Wright

by Nelson Algren

Richard Wright came to Chicago because there was no other place for him to go. He came as a stranger, lived as a stranger, and he left without looking back. "Whenever I leave that town I feel as though I had been in a three-day nightmare," he wrote from Mexico in 1940.

Yet his impact upon Chicago has been more enduring than that of any merchant prince, mayor or newspaper owner. For his impact was not upon City Hall but upon the city's conscience; and therefore upon the conscience of humanity.

Beginning himself as a face without a name among a multitude of nameless faces, an inarticulate man of no address, a being entitled to survive but possessing no claim to an individuality of his own, he became the voice of multitudes now claiming not merely an address, but their individuality as men. His voice opened a wedge for the inarticulate of the world, both black and white.

The challenge Wright raised was both specific and general. In *Native Son* he asserted specifically that, when a crime is committed by a man who has been excluded from civilization, civilization is accomplice to the crime. In defense of Bigger Thomas he demanded of the prosecution: "Let's see your hands."

More generally, he asserted that any man who exists without society's recognizing him as a unique being, is dehumanized, a mere thing. And he said this to Negroes as well as to whites.

"I really think Negroes are to blame for the reactions to *Native Son*," he wrote, "so few of them have ever tried to tell the truth about how they feel. They are shamed, scared and want to save their pride. Well, in writing that book I just threw shame, fear and pride out of the window."

"I knew I'd never get to be twenty-one anyhow," a teen-ager once assured a Chicago judge upon being sentenced to the electric chair. He also meant, "Let's see your hands."

"I never knew I was alive in this world until I felt things hard enough to kill for them," Bigger Thomas explains himself in the final scene of *Native Son*, "But I'm all right now." He meant that he had joined the company of men by the only means men had left him. He had made it, too.

Wright knew that in both of these youths the need to belong to the company of men had been strong enough to kill for that recognition. He knew this firsthand. *Native Son* is the emotional autobiography of a man who refused to be either a thing or a criminal. Bigger Thomas forced recognition by an act of murder, Wright by an act of art.

He went for truth first to the respectable and the articulate, but their answers were false. So he went where Dostoevski, Dreiser, Darrow and Farrell had gone for truth—to the born-to-be-doomed.

Today the walls of that death house where Bigger Thomas clung are widening, to reveal multitudes born-to-be-doomed, asking now, "Doomed by whom?"

The multitudes of the tin-roofed Hoovervilles of Caracas, the men and women burning passes that stamp them as mere things in Johannesburg, the Cuban peasants from the fields—these are not overturning our world upon instruction from the Kremlin, but from the instruction of their own spirits assuring them that they, too, belong to the company of men.

The accusation Dick Wright spoke as a prophecy has turned, two decades later, into a warning:

"Let's see your hands."

Chronology of Important Dates

	Wright	The Age
1908	Born in Natchez, Mississippi, September 4.	Mass unemployment results from Panic of 1907; founding of "Ash Can School" of art; Arnold Bennett's *The Old Wives' Tale*.
1909		Founding of the NAACP.
1912		James Weldon Johnson's *The Autobiography of an Ex-Colored Man*.
1920–29		The Harlem Literary Renaissance.
1923		Jean Toomer's *Cane*.
1927	Moves from Mississippi to the South Side of Chicago.	Flight of Charles Lindbergh from New York to Paris; Teapot Dome Scandal; execution of Sacco and Vanzetti; Broadway production of *Show Boat*.
1930		Langston Hughes's *Not Without Laughter*.
1932	Joins the Communist Party.	Election of Franklin D. Roosevelt as president; staggering level (13 million) of unemployment; National Convention of the Communist Party in Chicago; Aldous Huxley's *Brave New World*; William Faulkner's *Light in August*.

1933	Elected executive secretary of the John Reed Club in Chicago.	Launching of the New Deal by the Roosevelt administration; Gertrude Stein's *The Autobiography of Alice B. Toklas*; André Malraux's *La Condition Humaine.*
1934	Begins work on *Lawd Today* (published posthumously).	Hitler becomes Führer of Germany. Stalin begins purges of the Russian Communist Party. Arnold Toynbee's *A Study of History*; F. Scott Fitzgerald's *Tender Is the Night.*
1937	Receives *Story* magazine's best short story of the year prize for "Fire and Cloud," the last story in *Uncle Tom's Children.*	
1938	*Uncle Tom's Children* (four novellas) published.	Passage of the Wage and Hours Act, which increased the minimum wage and reduced the basic work week.
1940	*Native Son* published; *Uncle Tom's Children* reissued with addition of "The Ethics of Living Jim Crow" and "Bright and Morning Star." Receives Spingarn Medal of the National Association for the Advancement of Colored People; marries Dhima Meadman (whom he left the following year).	Winston Churchill becomes prime minister of Great Britain. Fall of France; passage in the United States of the Selective Service Act; W. E. B. Du Bois's *Dusk of Dawn*; Ernest Hemingway's *For Whom the Bell Tolls.*
1941	*12 Million Black Voices: A Folk History of the Negro in the United States* published; marries Ellen Poplar.	Japanese attack on Pearl Harbor; U.S. entry into World War II; Sherwood Anderson dies.
1944	Leaves the Communist Party, feeling it no longer	D-day landing in Normandy; Communist Party of the

	champions civil rights; "I Tried to Be a Communist" published.	United States dissolved, its leaders form the Communist Political Association.
1945	*Black Boy* published.	Dropping of the atomic bomb on Hiroshima and Nagasaki; surrender of Germany and Japan.
1946	Moves to France at the invitation of the French government (and over the objection of the American government).	Beginning of the Nuremberg War Trials; André Gide's *Journal, 1939–42*; Eugene O'Neill's *The Iceman Cometh*.
1952		Ralph Ellison's *Invisible Man*.
1953	*The Outsider* published; makes trip to Africa.	Inauguration of President Dwight D. Eisenhower; Senator Joseph McCarthy charges Soviet espionage activities in the United States; James Baldwin's *Go Tell It on the Mountain*.
1954	*Savage Holiday* (a novel) and *Black Power* (a bitterly received report on the African journey) published.	Dr. K. Nkrumah forms government of the Gold Coast; award of Nobel Prize for Literature to Ernest Hemingway. Racial segregation in U.S. public schools banned by Supreme Court.
1955	Makes journey through Spain.	Samuel Beckett's *Waiting for Godot*.
1956	*The Color Curtain: A Report on the Bandung Conference* and *Pagan Spain* (a report on observations in Spain) published.	In South Africa mass arrests of Europeans and Africans on treason charges; Negro bus boycott led by Dr. Martin Luther King, Jr., leads Supreme Court to declare segregation on buses and streetcars unconstitutional. Autherine Lucy, first black, enrolls at University of Alabama.

1957	*White Man, Listen!* (a collection of lectures and essays on what Du Bois called "the problem of the twentieth century—the color line") published.	U.S. paratroopers sent to Central High School in Little Rock, Ark., to protect 9 black students enrolled in the previously all-white school; Jack Kerouac's *On the Road*.
1958	*The Long Dream*, a poorly received novel, published.	Governor Orval E. Faubus of Arkansas defies Supreme Court ruling against segregation by closing four high schools in Little Rock; first U.S. earth satellite, *Explorer*, launched; J. K. Galbraith's *The Affluent Society*.
1959		Lorraine Hansberry's *A Raisin in the Sun*.
1960	Dies of a heart attack in a special clinic in Paris on November 28.	Shooting of 67 Africans at Sharpeville during a demonstration against South African apartheid; the Congo crisis; John F. Kennedy elected president of the United States; a civil rights bill passed by the Senate; only 6 percent of the schools in the South integrated; Felton Turner, a 27-year-old Negro, lynched in Texas.
1961	*Eight Men* (a collection of both new works and early works—"The Man Who Lived Underground," 1942, and "Almos' a Man," 1941) published.	Army revolt in Algeria; withdrawal of South Africa from the British Commonwealth; foundation of the Republic of the Congo; "Freedom Riders" attacked at Anniston and Birmingham, Alabama; "Sit-in Movement" begins when black college students refuse to leave a lunch counter in Greensboro, N.C.; Ernest Hemingway dies.

Notes on the Editor and Contributors

HOUSTON A. BAKER, JR., editor of this volume, is Associate Professor of English at the University of Virginia, Charlottesville. He has taught Black American Literature at Yale University and is the editor of *Black Literature in America*. His collection of essays, *Long Black Song: Essays in Black American Literature and Culture*, was published by the University Press of Virginia in 1972.

NELSON ALGREN, who now lives in Chicago, has received a number of awards for his fiction. His novels include *Somebody in Roots, The Man With the Golden Arm*, and *A Walk on the Wild Side*.

JAMES BALDWIN is one of the most outstanding artistic activists of the present day. His novels include *Go Tell It on the Mountain* and *Another Country*, and he has written drama and essays. *Notes of A Native Son* (1955), his first collection of essays, established his reputation as a writer.

ROBERT A. BONE is Professor of Literature at Teachers College, Columbia University. He is well known for his study of black American fiction *The Negro Novel in America* and for his work on the novels of James Baldwin.

MALCOLM COWLEY has served as associate editor for the *New Republic* and since 1948 has been literary adviser for The Viking Press. As poet, translator, essayist, and critic, Cowley has been prolific. His works include *The Literary Situation, Blue Juniata, Think Back on Us*, and most recently, *A Many-Windowed House: Collected Essays on American Writers and American Writing*.

DOROTHY CANFIELD FISHER (1879–1958) was a Vermont novelist who produced works on her home state and accounts of famous Americans of her acquaintance. Her writings include: *The Bent Twig, The Brimming Cup, Four Square* (short stories), and *Vermont Tradition: The Biography of an Outlook on Life*.

DONALD B. GIBSON has taught at Wayne State University and served as Fulbright Lecturer in American Literature at Jagiellonian University, Cracow, Poland. He is presently Associate Professor of American Literature at the University of Connecticut, Storrs. His critical study *The Fiction of*

Stephen Crane appeared in 1968, and since then he has edited *Five Black Writers.*

IRVING HOWE, author, historian, and critic, has taught literature at Brandeis University, Stanford University, and Hunter College. He has served as editor of *Dissent* and written a number of well-known critical studies such as *Sherwood Anderson: A Critical Biography, William Faulkner: A Critical Study,* and *Politics and the Novel.*

GEORGE E. KENT, a native of Columbus, Georgia, has lectured on Richard Wright at a number of colleges and universities. He is currently Professor of English at the University of Chicago.

DAN MCCALL has been a member of the English Department faculty at Cornell University since 1966. His works include a novel, *The Man Says Yes* (1969).

Selected Bibliography

ABCARIAN, RICHARD, *Richard Wright's Native Son, A Critical Handbook.* Belmont, California: Wadsworth Publishing Company, Inc., 1970. The book constitutes a fine document. It includes background accounts, related essays, and an extended bibliography.

BRIGNANO, CARL, *Richard Wright: An Introduction to the Man and His Work.* Pittsburgh: University of Pittsburgh Press, 1970. The book is a useful introduction to some of Wright's works, but it is plagued by factual errors and an awkward style.

BRYER, JACKSON R., "Richard Wright (1908–1960): A Selected Checklist of Criticism," *Wisconsin Studies in Contemporary Literature,* I (1960), 22–33. This list includes short annotations on primary works, articles, newspaper accounts of Wright and his canon, and reviews of the major works.

BURGUM, EDWIN BERRY, "The Promise of Democracy in Richard Wright's *Native Son,*" in *The Novel and the World's Dilemma.* New York: Russell and Russell, 1963, pp. 223–40. The author feels that *Native Son* continues the protest tradition of black American fiction, illustrates the shortcomings of American democratic ideals in the life of the common black man, and expresses a new mood among black writers and the black masses.

CREEKMORE, HERBERT, "Social Factors in *Native Son,*" *University Review,* VIII (1941), 136–43. The article treats the novel as proletarian fiction and states that the social message is distorted by the romantic and "thriller" elements of the work.

ELLISON, RALPH, "The World and the Jug," in *Shadow and Act.* New York: Random House, 1964, pp. 115–47. Ellison's essay is an answer to Irving Howe's "Black Boys and Native Sons," and it sets Richard Wright in a broad cultural perspective.

EMANUEL, JAMES A., "Fever and Feeling: Notes on the Imagery of *Native Son,*" *Negro Digest,* XVIII (1968), 16–26. This is one article in a special issue of *Negro Digest* (now *Black World*) on Richard Wright, and is a listing of the major images in *Native Son,* such as snow, walls, the furnace, crucifixion, and claustrophobia.

GIBSON, DONALD B., "Richard Wright: A Bibliographical Essay," *CLA Journal*, XII (1969), 360–65. The essay includes a listing of bibliographies of Wright's works, editions, biographies, criticism, and influences, along with insightful comments.

KINNAMON, KENETH, "*Native Son:* The Personal, Social, and Political Background," *Phylon*, XXX, 66–72. The article is a survey of biographical and sociohistorical factors, such as the trial of Robert Nixon in Chicago, that may have influenced the writing of *Native Son*.

MARGOLIES, EDWARD, *The Art of Richard Wright*. Carbondale: Southern Illinois University Press, 1969. The work constitutes a useful introduction to Wright, and it includes a discussion of "three types of revolution" in *Native Son*.

REDDING, SAUNDERS, "The Alien Land of Richard Wright," in *Soon One Morning*, ed. Herbert Hill. New York: Alfred A. Knopf, Inc., 1965, pp. 50–59. The author believes that Wright's artistic fires were extinguished by his expatriation in France.

SCOTT, NATHAN A., "Search for Beliefs: Fiction of Richard Wright," *University of Kansas City Review*, XXIII (1956), 19–24 and 131–38. The essay is a discussion of Wright's philosophical development four years prior to his death.